M000111702

STRESS AND RELAXATION

a consultation with **DR VERNON COLEMAN**

STRESS AND RELAXATION

HAMLYN

NOTE

THIS BOOK IS NOT INTENDED AS AN ALTERNATIVE TO PERSONAL, PROFESSIONAL MEDICAL ADVICE. THE READER SHOULD CONSULT A PHYSICIAN IN ALL MATTERS RELATING TO HEALTH, AND PARTICULARLY IN RESPECT OF ANY SYMPTOMS WHICH MAY REQUIRE DIAGNOSIS OR MEDICAL ATTENTION. WHILE THE ADVICE AND INFORMATION ARE BELIEVED TO BE ACCURATE AND TRUE AT THE TIME OF GOING TO PRESS, NEITHER THE AUTHOR NOR THE PUBLISHER CAN ACCEPT ANY LEGAL RESPONSIBILITY OR LIABILITY FOR ANY ERRORS OR OMISSIONS THAT MAY BE MADE

FIRST PUBLISHED IN GREAT BRITAIN 1993
BY HAMLYN, AN IMPRINT OF REED CONSUMER BOOKS LIMITED,
MICHELIN HOUSE, 81 FULHAM ROAD, LONDON SW3 6RB
AND AUCKLAND, MELBOURNE, SINGAPORE AND TORONTO

COPYRIGHT © VERNON COLEMAN 1993
DESIGN AND ILLUSTRATIONS © REED INTERNATIONAL BOOKS LIMITED
1993

ISBN 0 600 57524 1

A CIP RECORD FOR THIS BOOK IS AVAILABLE AT THE BRITISH LIBRARY

PRINTED IN CHINA

CONTENTS

CHAPTER ONE

The Causes Of Stress

We live in strange, difficult and confusing times. In some ways – largely material – we are richer than any of our ancestors. In other ways – largely spiritual – we are infinitely poorer.

Most of us live in well-equipped homes that our great-grandparents would marvel at. We have access to (relatively) clean drinking water at the turn of a tap. At the flick of a switch, we can obtain light to work by and heat to cook by. We have automatic ovens, washing machines, tumble driers, dish washers, food blenders, vacuum cleaners, television sets, video recorders and a whole host of other devices designed either to make our working lives easier, or our leisure hours longer or more enjoyable. We can travel thousands of miles in a matter of hours.

"We have created a world in which we cannot cope without artificial aids, and loneliness, unhappiness, anxiety and depression are now more common than at any previous time in our history"

We are surrounded by the gaudy signs of our wealth and the physical consequence of human ambition and endeavour, but we have become so dependent on artefacts that when they break down we become aggressive and irritable. We have created a world in which we cannot cope without artificial aids, and loneliness, unhappiness, anxiety and depression are now more common than at any previous time in our history. Never before has there been so much sadness, dissatisfaction and frustration as there is today. The demand for tranquillizers and sleeping tablets has steadily increased as our national and individual wealth has increased.

We have access to sophisticated communications systems and we have far more power over our environment than our ancestors ever had; yet we are regularly reminded of our vulnerability and our dependence on the system we have created. We are materially wealthy but spiritually deprived. We have conquered most of our planet and some of the space which surrounds it, but we are woefully unable to live peacefully with one another.

As we become materially richer so we also seem to become more fearful and spiritually poorer. The more we acquire, the more we seem to need, and the more we learn, the greater our ignorance. The more control we have over our environment, the more damage we do to it. The more successful we become, the more miserable we are. The more we learn, the more we forget about our duties and responsibilities to one another.

As manufacturers and advertisers have deliberately translated our wants into needs, so we have exchanged generosity and caring for greed and self-concern. Politicians and teachers, scientists and parents have encouraged each succeeding generation to convert simple dreams and aspirations into fiery no-holds-barred ambitions. In the name of progress we have sacrificed goodwill, common sense and thoughtfulness and the gentle, the weak and the warm-hearted have been trampled upon by hordes who think only of the future. Our society is a sad one; the cornerstones of our world are selfishness, greed, anger and hatred. Those are the driving forces which society teaches us to respect.

During the last 50 or so years, we have changed our world beyond recognition. With the aid of psychologists, clever advertising copywriters have learned to exploit our weaknesses and fears and our natural apprehensions to help create demands for new and increasingly expensive products. Our world has changed dramatically. Tradition, dignity, craftsmanship, values and virtues have been pushed aside in the search for greater productivity and profitability.

It is hardly surprising that all these changes have produced new stresses and strains. The pressures to succeed, to conform and to acquire, ensure that the base levels of daily stress are fixed at dangerously high levels.

TOXIC STRESS

Each one of us faces stress. Everywhere you look you come face to face with individual and personal stresses. There are stresses in your business life and stresses in your social life. These are the sort of basic, apparently simple, stresses which develop when you cannot afford to pay your gas bill, when your car won't start on a cold winter's morning and when you find yourself faced with too many responsibilities.

Theoretically, these are stresses that you can easily do something about. You can choose to avoid them if you want to. You can confront them or control them. You can share them or deal with them yourself. You have some freedom of action because these are personal stresses.

But many of these stresses are not as easily avoided as you might imagine them to be because, although they sound as though they are under your control, they are not. To a large extent, these stresses are created by pressures which are an integral part of the world around you.

It is for this reason that I call the result of these pressures 'toxic stress' (this is a term that I have devised to describe this very particular type of stress). These stresses cannot be avoided completely (although your exposure to them and the damage they do can be controlled); they produce frustrations which are difficult to define; they produce bitterness and they produce a deep and enduring sense of ill-defined, unexplained despair.

For 20 years it has been recognized that stress plays a vital part in the development of most illnesses but today the fastest growing illness in the world is what I call 'The Twentieth Century Blues' (see also page 46) – a largely unrecognized problem that already affects one person in three and is spreading rapidly. The Twentieth Century Blues is caused by 'toxic stress'.

Toxic stress is far more destructive than ordinary stress. It is created – often deliberately – by politicians, lawyers and advertisers and it is the cause of much bitterness and many frustrations. It is the cause of the deep sense of ill-defined, inexplicable despair that is typical of victims of The Twentieth Century Blues.

Toxic stress is the type of stress that is produced by advertisements which make you feel incompetent or inadequate ('You're a failure if you can't afford to dress like this', 'You're a terrible parent if you don't buy X or Y for your children'), and it is the type of stress that is produced by lawyers who regard justice as an outdated concept and create laws which mean that however just your cause may be, you can't win.

The more thoughtful and imaginative you are, the more you are likely to be a victim of toxic stress and a sufferer from The Twentieth Century Blues. If you suffer from this disorder you are probably unusually sensitive, considerate and caring. You suffer because you are conscientious, honourable, hard-working, punctilious and honest. Your physical symptoms could include headaches, skin rashes, and indigestion. You are likely to suffer from problems as varied as irritable bowel syndrome and premenstrual tension. And you will be vulnerable to mental symptoms which will include sleeplessness and panic attacks.

The stresses created by the society in which you live are responsible for much of the stress which creates sadness, misery and despair. It is the existence of these high levels of toxic stress which helps to explain why individual attempts to deal with stress are often ineffective. It is the existence of toxic stress which explains why millions of people who believe that they have the stress in their lives under control are, nevertheless, suffering from stress-related disorders.

In a later chapter I will explain the driving forces such as guilt and ambition which are created by toxic stresses, but here I want simply to explain how toxic stresses are created.

THE PRESSURE OF ADVERTISING

Whatever else you do with your life you will always be a consumer. To the people who make items as varied as motor cars, refrigerators, underwear, indigestion remedies, biscuits, coat hangers and kitchen sinks you are a consumer. To lawyers, accountants, surveyors, house agents and even doctors you are a consumer.

In order to persuade you to become a customer, the people who provide these products and services spend considerable amounts of money trying to convince you that their products or services are better than anyone else's and are essential for a happy life.

ARE YOU SUFFERING FROM DEPRESSION?

IT IS IMPORTANT TO REMEMBER THAT THE CONDITION WHICH I HAVE DESCRIBED AS 'THE TWENTIETH CENTURY BLUES' IS VERY DIFFERENT TO DEPRESSION. SOME TYPES OF DEPRESSION MAY BE PRODUCED BY CHEMICAL CHANGES WITHIN YOUR BODY AND YOUR DOCTOR MAY BE ABLE TO HELP YOU. YOU SHOULD SEE YOUR DOCTOR AS SOON AS YOU CAN IF:

• YOU FEEL DEPRESSED

• YOU WAKE UP EARLY EVERY MORNING

• YOU HAVE LOST YOUR APPETITE

• YOU HAVE LOST WEIGHT (WITHOUT INTENDING TO)

• YOU ARE WORRIED ABOUT YOUR PHYSICAL OR MENTAL HEALTH

• YOU SUFFER FROM PHYSICAL SYMPTOMS WHICH YOU CANNOT EXPLAIN

• YOU SUSPECT THAT YOU MAY BE SUFFERING FROM A PHYSICAL OR MENTAL CONDITION REQUIRING TREATMENT

Advertisements dominate our lives

Every day your custom is solicited in a thousand different ways – some crude and some subtle. Every day you are bombarded with advertisements telling you to buy one of these and begging you to buy some of those, and explaining why your life will be incomplete if you do not spend your money on a little of this and a little of that. The pressure is remorseless and unremitting.

The professionals who prepare the advertisements with which you are confronted each day are only too aware of the fact that it is no longer enough for them to tell you the value of the product they are selling. These days, the competition is so great that advertising agencies are no longer content to tell you how to satisfy your basic needs. These days, advertising agencies know very well that in order to succeed in the modern market place they must create new needs; they know that their advertising must, through a mixture of exaggeration and deceit and through exploiting your fears and your weaknesses, create wants and desires, hopes and aspirations and to then turn those wants, desires, hopes and aspirations into needs.

Modern advertising agencies know (because they have done the necessary research) that it is impossible to sell anything to a satisfied man. But, in order to keep the money coming in, the advertising agencies must constantly encourage us to buy and they constantly need to find better ways to sell us goods and services that we do not really need.

Any fool can sell a product or a service that people need. If your shoes wear out then you will buy new ones or have the old ones repaired. If you are hungry and there is only one restaurant for miles then that restaurant will get your service. If your car is about to run out of petrol then a garage doesn't need to offer you free products to get your custom.

As far as the advertising agencies are concerned, the trick is to get you to buy shoes when you don't need to and to buy shoes that are more expensive than they need be; to buy food when you are not hungry and to fill your car with petrol long before its tank is empty, simply because you are attracted by the offer that accompanies a particular brand of fuel.

As far as the advertising industry is concerned, the basic trick is to turn your most ephemeral wants into basic needs. In order to do this advertising agencies use all their professional skills to make you dissatisfied with what you already have. They need you to be constantly dissatisfied and frustrated.

Modern advertising is a scientifically based creative art which is designed to raise the intensity of your desires and build your dissatisfaction and your fears. The advertising copywriter is hired to create unhappiness. Advertising is, in short, an industry which only works when it puts you under unnecessary stress.

Modern advertising is designed to make you dissatisfied with anything which isn't profitable. Advertising copywriters want to take away your appreciation of the simple things in life because they know that there is more profit in making things more complicated, more expensive and more unreliable. They want you to be in so much of a hurry that you eat instant foods rather than growing and preparing your own vegetables. They want you to ride in a car rather than walk or ride a bicycle. They want to make you feel guilty if you don't smell right or don't buy the right breakfast cereal for your children. They want you to feel a failure if you don't have the latest clothes on your back and the latest gadgets in your home.

Advertising is most successful when it persuades

you to forget your real needs and to replace them with wants; there is no doubt that the advertising industry is responsible for much of the sickness and much of the unhappiness in our society.

Even if you do buy the products they want to sell you, you will still not find the satisfaction that they promise you for the advertisements are shallow and the promises hollow. Whatever exaggerated claims they make you will be disappointed.

Your sex life will not suddenly improve just because you change your perfume or deodorant. Your social life will not change because you buy the latest clothes. You will not be immune to traffic jams just because you buy a new car with metallic paint and electric windows.

The advertising professionals make many promises which they know they cannot keep and whatever claims they make the chances are that you will remain frustrated and even more dissatisfied than you were before you spent your money. Your hopes and expectations will be aroused and then disappointed.

To the spiritual and mental frustration created by all this disappointment you must add physical frustration, too, for the chances are high that the product you buy will soon fail. Obsolescence is in-built and is essential to all new products. Built in mechanical or fashionable obsolescence enables the car companies to keep making and selling us new cars even though most of us already have relatively new vehicles parked outside

our homes. You might think you change your car because you want something more reliable or more comfortable but you probably don't: the chances are that you change your car because the advertising copywriters have succeeded in persuading you that your present vehicle is out of date and unfashionable.

Even if you don't have the money to spend on new cars, kitchen furniture, clothes and other goods so cleverly advertised, you will not escape. Advertising, designed to inflame your desires, will show you services you cannot buy and things you cannot have. It will create wants and then turn those wants into needs. Advertising creates frustration and disappointment, envy and dissatisfaction. If you are too poor to buy the things which are advertised, you will never discover that the products on offer are unlikely to satisfy the promises made for them.

Advertising is, without a doubt, one of the greatest causes of stress and is one of the greatest of modern threats to physical and mental health. Advertising agencies kill far more people than do industries which pollute the atmosphere.

Advertising is the symbol of modern society; it represents false temptations, hollow hopes and unhappiness and disenchantment; it inspires values which are based on fear and greed.

The pressure to win can produce damaging stress

HOW FEAR CREATES STRESS

Our ancestors lived in a world about which they understood very little and where they were constantly in danger. They had many things to be afraid of: death, pain, starvation and being eaten alive by wild animals to mention but four.

We, in contrast, should lead relatively fear-free lives; but all the evidence firmly shows that fear plays a much bigger part in our lives than it ever played in the lives of our ancestors. Why?

Probably because society needs us to be frightened. Fear is a powerful driving force which helps to push us forwards. Fear encourages us to accept things we do not like, to do work we do not enjoy and to spend money on things we neither want nor need. Fear cripples us but keeps us compliant.

It is not by accident that countless groups – politicians, commentators, experts, industries and advertising agencies – all deliberately do what they can to keep us

Fear is often used by politicians in search of power; extreme right-wing South African leader Eugene Terre Blanche addresses a rally

afraid. When did you last hear a politician, pundit or expert offering undiluted comfort and reassurance?

Fear is one of the most potent of all forces and it used to control us and to manipulate our emotions. Consider health for example.

You are encouraged to worry about your health in a thousand separate ways. Listen to the experts arguing about what is bad for you and you will soon feel twinges of fear nibbling at you. Most of the time your fears are created and maintained by people who have a vested, commercial interest in exploiting your fears so that they can sell you something.

The companies which make caffeine-free coffee tell you the virtues of drinking caffeine-free coffee – and warn you of the hazards of drinking ordinary coffee. The people who make low-fat products warn you of the hazards of eating products high in fat. Doctors frighten you into having regular health checks. Companies selling herbal remedies tell you how dangerous doctors can be. Companies making sweeteners warn you of the dangers of eating sugar. Companies involved in the marketing or distribution of sugar warn you of the danger of sugar substitutes.

You would not be normal if you were not constant-

ly afraid for your safety and constantly concerned about your health. Hypochondriasis is commonplace.

Fear is everywhere and is constantly used by people who want to manipulate you.

Politicians and police chiefs frighten you about street violence in order to encourage you to give them more power. Politicians make you frightened of your enemies abroad for the same reason. Television and radio means that you can be frightened more speedily and more effectively than ever before. Fear helps our society to sustain itself and to increase its power.

THE INJUSTICE OF THE LAW

Much unhappiness and frustration is caused by the fact that in our society the law is commonly confused with justice, liberty, freedom and equality.

In truth, the law has very little to do with these fundamental moral principles. The law exists to help society defend itself; it is used by those who represent society as a weapon with which to dominate and discriminate against individual powers and freedoms. The law is man's inadequate attempt to turn justice – an abstract theoretical concept – into practical reality. Sadly, it is invariably inspired more by the prejudices and self-interest of the law makers than by respect or concern for the rights of innocent individuals.

These misconceptions about the purpose of our law lead to much disappointment. And these misconceptions are partly to blame for a considerable amount of underlying stress.

No society has ever had as many laws as we have and yet few societies can have ever had less justice.

Many of the laws which exist today were created not to protect individuals or communities, but to protect the system. It is because such crimes threaten the security and sanctity of the system that theft and fraud often attract harsher sentences than crimes such as rape and murder which affect individuals, whose rights are seen as less significant.

The irony is that although the law was originally introduced to protect individuals and their property and to reduce their stresses, the law has itself become a tyrant and a major cause of stress. Today few individuals can afford to take advantage of the protection offered by the law. The law oppresses the weak, the poor and the powerless and sustains itself and the powers which preserve it. The enormous costs of litigation mean that there is one law for the rich and no law at all for the poor. The result is that the law threatens and reduces the rights of the weak and strengthens and augments the rights of the rich and powerful.

Things are made worse by the fact that the people employed by society to uphold and administer the law on behalf of the ordinary people too often take advantage of their positions to abuse their powers. The interpretation of the law is so often at the discretion of those who are paid to uphold it that those who have been hired by society become the law itself; neatly and effectively society protects itself against threat and bypasses the rights of individual citizens.

Too often, society allows officers of the courts to abuse their power in order to satisfy their own personal ambitions, grievances and prejudices. In return, society in its broadest and most undemocratic and domineering sense, is protected by the people who benefit from its patronage. It is the worst sort of symbiotic relationship, and the stress it produces is inescapable.

The final irony is that as respect for the law (and those hired to uphold it) diminishes, so the divide between the law and justice grows ever wider.

When people who are given the power to protect society disapprove of something which threatens their status, they introduce a new law. As political parties come and go so we accumulate layer after layer of new laws. It doesn't matter if the new laws conflict with the old laws as long as all the laws help to strengthen the status of the state.

Meanwhile, as the oppression of individuals continues, lawlessness (and disrespect for the law) grows among officials and those in power. Brutality, arrogance, corruption and hypocrisy have all damaged public faith in the law but the only response from society has been to create new laws to outlaw disapproval. Society's primary interest is to protect itself and society is not concerned with justice, freedom or equality since those are values which are appreciated only by individuals. Those who have power are concerned only with their own survival and with perpetuating their power. The simple truth is that we live in a corrupt society which creates countless stresses for ordinary people.

THE PERILS OF PROGRESS

Much of the stress from which we all suffer is created by our constant determination to progress.

Without progress industry would slow down, economic growth would be stifled and society would stand still. But without progress we would have time to enjoy our world and our lives; without progress we would be able to find happiness, contentment and stability. Without progress the structure of our society would not increase in importance and the power of those who regulate our lives would not be increased.

Progress does not always mean that things – and life – are better than they used to be

The truth is that we have created a world and a society which now controls us. Our present and our future are controlled by the social structure we have devised. Our institutions and establishments need progress in order to create and gain more power. We like to blame an invisible 'them' for our graceless state but there is no invisible 'them'. The power in our world is now vested in the institutions themselves. It is the structure of our society which controls us and in order to grow the structure needs progress.

While in order to help maintain and build the social structure which gives them their power and their authority, the individuals who work for institutions and organizations and parts of the establishment readily insist that progress is vital. They know that without progress their part of the social structure, and therefore their personal status, will decline. They know that in order to survive they must keep their institution alive and strong. And that means progress. The men and women who work for big companies know that without progress their companies will decline and lose power. The more power an individual has, the greater his interest in and support for progress will be.

They tell us that progress is vital and good but they are lying. They tell us that it is impossible to halt progress but they are lying. What they really mean is that progress is good for business or that progress offers some advantage in terms of money or power to the part of the social structure to which they are tied. Progress is, ironically, essential to the status quo.

Inevitably, anyone who works for an institution or large company will insist that progress means 'better'. It doesn't. Progress means that people change and it means that people have to work harder and take life more seriously and it means more stress. Progress means that things become more complicated and more likely to go wrong. Progress means that the things which you bought yesterday (and were happy with until the advertisers convinced you that they were out of date) are outdated and useless within months. Progress means that new is always better and that the future is always going to be better than the past.

Progress means that more and more people have to exchange a rich and varied, wholesome and healthy lifestyle for one which is hollow and filled with despair and loneliness. Progress means deprivation for people but strength for our social structures. Progress means that the jobs people do become more boring and less satisfying. Progress means more power to machines and computers. Progress means that things are more likely to go wrong. Progress means more destruction, more misery and more tedium. Progress means more damage to our planet. And, above all, progress means more stress, more pain, more anxiety and more illness.

Those who worship at the altar of progress make two simple but vital errors. They assume that man must always take full advantage of every new development and invention. And that he must always search for a better way of tackling everything he does.

Neither of these two assumptions is soundly based.

Just because man invents computers, supersonic jets and atomic bombs does not mean that he has to *use* these things regardless of the consequences.

Those who believe wholeheartedly in progress believe that we must always use every nugget of information we obtain. They believe that if man invents a way of travelling faster, then that way must be better than the old ways. They believe that if man invents a quicker and more effective way to kill people then he must use this more effective weapon. They believe that if a man invents a faster way of doing something, then that must inevitably be better. These assumptions are not logical although we often act as though they are.

Progress for the sake of progress often simply means change for the sake of change. Change is not always for the better. Nor is there much sense in the belief that man must always look for better ways to do things. The problem lies largely with the definition of the word 'better'. What exactly does it mean?

Is a television set better than a radio? Is a motor car better than a bicycle? Is an aeroplane better than a yacht? Is artificial turf better than real grass? Are artificial flowers better than the real thing?

Too often, progress simply means more frustration and more unhappiness. It means that we become more dependent on strangers and less capable of coping with daily crises. Progress means a loss of independence.

Are people wiser, happier and more contented now that electric toothbrushes are available? Are faster cars more satisfying than old ones? Are people more at peace than their ancestors now that the compact disc player has been invented? How much did the telephone improve the quality of life?

The truth, of course, is something of a compromise. Some advances are good. Some new technology is helpful and does improve the quality of our lives. Some new developments reduce pain, suffering and stress.

Society, however, isn't interested in compromise.

Society needs uncontrolled progress in order to grow. And the people who acquire their power and their status and their wealth from those institutions do what they are expected to do. Our world is no longer controlled by people. Tragically, it is controlled by the very structure that we created.

The truth is that progress can be a boon as well as a burden. It would be as stupid to claim that all progress is bad as it is to claim that all progress is good. Progress is good when we use it for our benefit rather than allow it to rule our lives. Progress is neither good nor bad

For many people progress has taken away joy and replaced it with drudgery

unless we make it so by what we do or fail to do.

But we no longer choose between those aspects of progress which can be to our benefit and those which may be harmful. We accept all progress as inevitable and essential, and in doing so we put ourselves under ever-increasing amounts of stress. We allow progress to dominate our lives and we have abandoned our right to control our own destiny.

CHAPTER TWO

The Effects Of Stress

I regard stress as just about the biggest threat to your health that exists, and anxiety is one of the commonest, most troublesome and most worrying consequences. Together they are responsible for a huge number of symptoms and diseases. If you suffer from dermatitis, asthma, arthritis, angina, high blood pressure, backache, baldness, bed wetting, sleeplessness, indigestion, headaches, dizziness, diarrhoea, diabetes, depression, constipation, frequent colds, sexual problems, wheezing, migraines, premenstrual tension, psoriasis, heartburn, hay fever, gall bladder disease, gastritis or any one of a hundred other common disorders the chances are that even if stress isn't the only cause of your trouble, it is a major contributing factor.

"I regard stress as just about the biggest threat to your health that exists, and anxiety is one of the commonest, most troublesome and most worrying consequences"

A few years ago, the medical profession regarded stress as something rather puzzling but these days I doubt if there is a doctor anywhere who does not accept that stress – by which I mean anything that causes fear, anxiety, worry, apprehension, anger or even excitement – can cause quite genuine physical responses and very real diseases.

No one knows for sure exactly how many diseases are caused by stress but there can no longer be any real doubt that at least three quarters of all diseases are caused or made worse by stress and personally I believe that between 90 and 95% of all illnesses - and in that total I include those illnesses which aren't treated by doctors as well as those which are - can be blamed at least partly (and in some cases wholly) on stress. Since there are hundreds of diseases which are caused or made worse by stress and hundreds of millions of individuals who are susceptible to stress the different variations on this theme which exist is almost infinite.

But here, for example, are a few case histories which illustrate the sort of ways in which stress (in its many different forms) can produce very real symptoms of illness and disease. Some readers may be surprised that even children can suffer from stress.

STRESS AT SCHOOL CAUSES A BAD CASE OF ASTHMA

When I first met K she was in a terrible state. She was only ten but she had an extremely unpleasant case of eczema (a nasty skin complaint which produces redness, flaking skin and soreness) and she also had a severe case of asthma for which she had already been treated with various drugs at the local hospital.

It was the asthma which led to my being called out to see her one summer evening. K was lying on her bed wheezing desperately. K's mother had left the bedroom window open, and the moment I got out of my car outside her home I could hear her wheezing. It took a while to help improve her breathing and I thought I was going to have to get K admitted to hospital.

Eventually, however, K did stop wheezing and, exhausted, she drifted off to sleep. As I was going down the stairs her parents both spoke at once. They wanted to know if K would be fit to take an examination at school the following morning. K's father, in particular, seemed very worried about this. He told me that he believed that all tests and examinations needed to be taken seriously and that he very much wanted his daughter to be a success at school.

I told them that I would have to leave it to them to decide how well K was the following morning but that my feeling was that since she was only ten and had had a very disturbed night she might be better off spending the day resting at home. I felt slightly uneasy about all this. It seemed to me that K's parents were a touch too concerned about their daughter's school work and perhaps not concerned enough about her asthma.

The following morning I telephoned K's home to see how she was. Her mother told me that she had been well enough to go to school to take her examination. I said I was pleased about this but asked them to ring me again if there were any more problems. I also said that I would like to see and talk to K as soon as possible.

I saw K again sooner than I had hoped.

I was called to see her at home that afternoon. She was wheezing so heavily that this time I had to arrange for her to go into hospital.

When she came home I sat down with K and talked to her. It quickly became clear that she was very worried about her school work. Her parents had put her under an enormous amount of pressure to do well. She felt that if she did not come top in every test she would be failing them. And it was clear that the pressure was making her ill. Afterwards I talked to her parents and eventually succeeded in persuading them to be less demanding and to reduce their expectations. They agreed that they would try not to put K under any pressure for a few weeks to see what happened.

A month or so later, when I saw K next, she was much happier, healthier and fitter. Her wheezing had stopped, her eczema had cleared up and she looked much happier and brighter too. Much to her parents' surprise she was even doing better at school as well. They agreed to stop putting their daughter under so much pressure and K benefited enormously.

STRESS AT WORK CAUSES INDIGESTION

When J came into my surgery he looked edgy and uncomfortable. He looked at his watch as he sat down and he seemed to be in a hurry.

When I asked him to tell me what was troubling him he took an empty medicine bottle out of his pocket and handed it to me.

'Would you prescribe some of this for me?' he asked. 'I've been buying several bottles a week and it's very expensive.'

I looked at the label on the bottle. It was a proprietary antacid mixture - the sort that is widely sold to alleviate indigestion, gastritis and other stomach upsets.

'How long have you been taking it?' I asked him.

J shrugged. 'Months,' he said.

'Does it work?' was my next question.

'It used to work better than it does now,' he told me. 'I have to drink quite a lot of it now to have the same effect. I did try antacid tablets. They're more convenient but they don't work anywhere near as well.'

I asked J if he had any other symptoms. He told me that he sometimes felt sick, though he hadn't ever been sick, and that spicy or rich foods seemed to make his stomach pains considerably worse. 'Has anything been worrying you recently?' I asked him.

J laughed wryly. He then explained that he had recently been promoted to a new position by his firm. He was a salesman and as a result of his promotion he had, he told me, been given much greater responsibilities. His new position meant that he had to do a lot more travelling and was in charge of several other salesmen. He told me that all the extra work he had to do had played havoc with his home life and had meant that he no longer had time to play with his young children or to enjoy the sports he had previously enjoyed. He confessed that he had never before in his life felt quite so much under stress.

I told J that in order to make sure that he didn't have a peptic ulcer developing I needed to get some hospital tests done. I warned him that although I could probably 'cure' his pains with the aid of tablets the chances were high that the pains would simply come back again if he didn't change his lifestyle.

'Can you go back to doing the job you had before?' 'Oh, yes!' said J. 'But my present job pays much better. And I get a bigger car.'

He told me that he didn't really have time to talk any more because he had to drive two hundred miles to see a customer. He said he just wanted another prescription for his antacid medicine and that he didn't have the time to go to the hospital. He then picked up his empty bottle and angrily walked out of the surgery, ignoring my protests.

Although my last word to J had been to ask him to come back and see me again within a few days, whenever he had a moment to spare, I didn't see him again for nearly two months.

When I did see him next he was in our local hospital. He had collapsed while out on the road and been taken there by an ambulance. He was extremely lucky. The ulcer he had developed had burst and it could have killed him.

This brush with death frightened J into taking action. He agreed to give up his tiring and stressful job and to go back to his previous, happier, healthier (and poorer) lifestyle.

Stress had nearly killed him.

STRESS DURING A DIVORCE MAKES HER HAIR FALL OUT

When M came into the surgery I thought it was odd that she kept her hat on. Not many women wear a hat at all these days - even fewer keep their hats on indoors. But M did.

At first she didn't seem to want to tell me what was troubling her. She talked about the weather, the local news, and her sister who had just had a baby. She also talked about her divorce. It had been a particularly messy divorce but it had been over for a few months and she said that she thought she was over the worst.

Eventually, I asked M to tell me what it was that was troubling her.

'I'm going bald, doctor,' she told me. She took off her hat and sure enough I could see that several fairly clear bald patches had developed. 'My hair is just coming out in clumps,' she told me tearfully. 'Its got so that I daren't brush my hair any more, and I dread waking up in the morning because I know that there are going to be hairs all over the pillow.'

M was suffering from a condition called alopecia areata - a dramatic type of hair loss which can affect both men and women and which can occur at virtually any age (although it is believed to be most common among men and women in their teens and twenties). The hair loss is often so severe that many sufferers feel that they have to wear a wig to cover up their baldness.

On a normal, healthy head hair falls out at the rate of between sixty and ninety hairs a day. In alopecia areata hair falls out much faster than this - it really does come out in clumps sometimes. And there really are bald patches.

The odd thing about alopecia areata is that the loss of hair often takes place after the stress that causes it has occurred. The condition is caused by the fact that the hair roots just stop growing for a while and it then takes some time for the bald patches to appear.

Sadly, I had to tell M that there wasn't anything I could give her to make her hair grow back. But I did explain to her that in many cases the hair does start to grow back again by itself.

Alopecia areata is an unusual example of a stress induced disease because it only becomes apparent weeks or months after the incident which caused it.

DISEASES THAT CAN BE CAUSED BY STRESS

TO SEE JUST HOW MUCH STRESS AFFECTS YOUR LIFE MAKE A LIST OF THE DISEASES ON THESE TWO PAGES FROM WHICH YOU SUFFER NOW OR HAVE SUFFERED IN THE PAST

- ACCIDENT PRONENESS
- ADDICTION
- ALCOHOLISM
- ALLERGIC DERMATITIS
- ALLERGIC RHINITIS
- ALOPECIA (HAIR LOSS)
- ANAEMIA
- ANGINA PECTORIS
- ANKYLOSING SPONDYLITIS
- ANOREXIA
- ANXIETY
- APHTHOUS ULCERS
- APOPLEXY
- APPETITE LOSS
- ARRHYTHMIA
- ARTERIOSCLEROSIS
- ARTHRITIS
- ASTHMA

- BACKACHE
- BALDNESS
- BED WETTING
- BLOOD PRESSURE
- BREATHLESSNESS
- BRONCHITIS

- CANCER
- CARDIAC FAILURE
- CEREBRAL ARTERIOSCLEROSIS
- CEREBRAL HAEMORRHAGE
- CEREBRAL THROMBOSIS
- CHOLECYSTITIS
- COLDS

- COLITIS
- CONSTIPATION
- CYSTITIS
- DEPRESSION
- DERMATITIS
- DIABETES
- DIARRHOEA
- DIGESTIVE DISORDERS
- DIZZINESS
- DUODENAL ULCER
- DYSMENORRHOEA (PAINFUL PERIODS)
- DYSPEPSIA (INDIGESTION)
- DYSPHAGIA (DIFFICULTY IN SWALLOWING)

- ECZEMA
- ENURESIS (INCONTINENCE, BED WETTING)
- EPILEPSY

- FAINTING
- FEAR
- FLATULENCE
- FRIGIDITY

- GALL BLADDER DISEASE
- GALL STONES
- GASTRITIS
- GASTROENTERITIS
- GIDDINESS
- GOUT

- HABITUATION (OF DRUGS)
- HAIR LOSS
- HAY FEVER
- HEADACHES
- HEART ATTACK
- HEART BLOCK
- HEART FAILURE

HEARTBURN □
HEPATITIS □
HYPERTENSION □
HYPOCHONDRIASIS □
HYSTERIA □

IMPOTENCE □
INCONTINENCE □
INDIGESTION □
INFARCTION □
INFECTIVE DISEASES □
INFLUENZA □
INSOMNIA □
INTERMITTENT CLAUDICATION □
IRRITABILITY □
IRRITABLE BOWEL SYNDROME □
ISCHAEMIC HEART DISEASE □
ITCHING □

JOINT DISEASES □

LIBIDO LOSS □
LUMBAGO □

MARRIAGE PROBLEMS □
MEMORY FAILURE □
MENOPAUSAL PROBLEMS □
MENSTRUAL PROBLEMS □
MIGRAINE □
MYOCARDIAL INFARCTION □
MYXOEDEMA □

NAUSEA □
NERVOUS BREAKDOWN □
NIGHTMARES □

OBESITY □
OBSESSIONS □
OSTEOARTHRITIS □

PALPITATIONS □
PEPTIC ULCERATION □
PERSONALITY DISORDERS □
PHOBIAS □

POST BABY BLUES □
PREMENSTRUAL TENSION □
PSORIASIS □
PUERPERAL DEPRESSION □

REACTIVE DEPRESSION □
RHEUMATISM □

SCIATICA □
SEXUAL PROBLEMS □
SICKNESS □
SLEEPLESSNESS □
STAMMER □
STROKE □
STUTTER □
SUICIDE ATTEMPTS □

TENSION □
TREMORS □
TUMOURS □
THYROID TROUBLE □
THYROTOXICOSIS □

ULCERS □
ULCERATIVE COLITIS □

VOMITING □

WHEEZING □

NOTE: SOME OF THE DISORDERS LISTED HERE HAVE OTHER CAUSES IN ADDITION TO STRESS. BUT STRESS IS A COMMON CONTRIBUTORY CAUSE WHICH OFTEN ALSO EXACERBATES THE SYMPTOMS THAT ARE PRODUCED.

HEADACHES

Four out of every five people suffer from headaches. Most get their headaches irregularly. Some suffer daily. The headache is the most common single symptom people complain about – and stress is the most common cause.

Unfortunately, doctors don't always treat headaches very well, often sending you away with aspirin.

The main reason for this is that although headaches may be crippling they aren't usually life-threatening. Headaches can be excruciatingly painful and can wreck your life in many ways but they won't usually kill you; and doctors have a nasty habit of dismissing problems which make their patients' lives miserable but don't threaten to kill them.

Go and see your doctor with something rare and threatening and you will find yourself surrounded by expensive equipment and men in white coats before you can wince. But turn up with a skull-numbing headache and you will probably stagger out two minutes later clutching a prescription for 20 aspirin tablets.

But the good news is that most headaches can be tamed because they are caused by stress, pressure and anxiety and can, therefore, often be prevented.

A worry about something that has happened can produce as nervous headache – as can a worry about something that might happen in the future.

Strains caused by concentrating hard on something can cause exactly the same symptoms. If you have been crouched over the accounts, stuck in a tedious meeting, or hunched over a steering wheel then you are likely to develop a nervous headache.

You can see how the pains develop simply by looking at yourself in the mirror the next time you are worried about something. Look around your eyes – there will be worry lines developing there because you are frowning, squinting and screwing up your eyes. Look at the way your shoulders are hunched. The nervous tension in your body is producing muscle tension – and the muscle tension is causing your headache.

The headache will probably start in one place and gradually spread over the top of your head. It may be throbbing; it may feel as if you've got a hat on your head that is too tight; it may be a steady, pressing ache. It can last a few minutes to a week or more and may slowly spread to the muscles of your neck and your jaw. Every time you are upset or anxious or unhappy the pain will get worse.

Most people try to deal with headaches of this sort with aspirin or paracetamol. And since both are excellent drugs they will probably work.

But taking a painkilling tablet to cure a nervous headache is rather like pouring water into a car that has a burst radiator hose – it is a *very* short-term solution to a potentially long-term problem.

YOU MUST, OF COURSE, ALWAYS SEEK YOUR DOCTOR'S ADVICE ABOUT A HEADACHE – PARTICULARLY IF:

- IT FOLLOWS A HEAD INJURY
- IT IS SEVERE AND/OR HAS DEVELOPED SUDDENLY AND WITHOUT WARNING
- IT IS ACCOMPANIED BY A STIFF NECK
- YOU ALSO HAVE A TEMPERATURE
- IT LASTS FOR MORE THAN 24 HOURS
- YOU HAVE RECURRING HEADACHES
- IT DEVELOPS AFTER YOU HAVE STARTED MEDICAL TREATMENT
- YOU ARE WORRIED

HERE ARE A FEW SOLUTIONS THAT DO NOT INVOLVE PILLS.

1. Since muscle tension will be helping to make your headache worse you can help yourself by deliberately relaxing the muscles of your head and neck. This is not as difficult as it sounds.

Deliberately clench the muscles of your left hand. Try it now. Make the muscles go as tight as you can get them. Hold your fist in that position while you count up to 20. You will feel a pain developing. You can let your fist go loose now.

Much the same sort of thing happens in your head when you are under pressure. The muscles of your face, head and neck all become tight and so

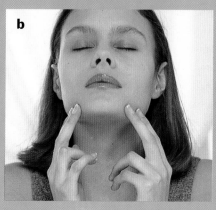

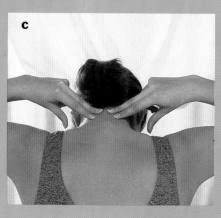

you get a pain. By learning how to relax the muscles around your head you can get rid of a headache.

You really need to practise this when you have not got a headache. Screw up your face really tightly. Try to tighten up every muscle in your face. Tense your neck. Try to get your whole head and neck feeling uncomfortably tight.

Now, slowly, relax all those muscles. Deliberately let them go all loose and floppy. You should be able to feel the tension and the potential pain pour out of them.

Practise this as often as you can. Then, next time you get a nervous headache you will be able to recognize the difference between tensed facial and neck muscles and relaxed face and neck muscles – and you will be able to combat your headache by deliberately letting your muscles go loose.

2. Next time you feel a nervous headache developing try to look at what is happening as objectively as you can. Try to put everything into perspective. Often when things go wrong we panic and worry ourselves sick when worrying really isn't going to help at all.

If you are 20 minutes late, sitting frowning in your traffic jam isn't going to help at all. It is just going to mean that when you finally get to your destination you will have a stinking headache and feel absolutely rotten.

Try to think of good things – things that you are looking forward to, or try to remember good times in the past.

3. Try massaging the muscles of your face and neck with your finger tips. Start at the outside of your eyes. Make little round circular movements with your finger tips (see figure **a**). Be slow and gentle. Then gradually work your way down the line of your jaw (see figure **b**). Next, massage the bridge of your nose between your thumb and first finger (see figure **c**). Then massage your forehead. Finally, use both hands to massage the back of your neck (see figure **d**). You will be amazed at how much difference it makes. Move your head forwards and backwards to get rid of some of the tension. Try moving it from side to side as well. Be gentle: do not make any sudden or painful movements.

HEADACHE SUFFERERS ARE OBSESSIONAL!

It has long been argued by some researchers that people who suffer a lot from headaches tend to be exceptionally obsessional.

The argument is that individuals who worry a lot about getting things absolutely right and who are meticulous and neat are far more likely to suffer from the sort of localized muscle tensions which can – and frequently do – lead to the development of headaches.

I receive an enormous amount of mail from readers around the world and I have noticed that the letters which come in confirm this association between obsessive neatness and headaches.

It is not so much the content of the letters that I have found convincing as the style in which the letters have been written and presented.

The vast majority of letters from headache sufferers are very neatly written, many in block capitals, and many letters come with a neatly typed self-addressed envelope or gummed label.

From this spontaneous but quite large survey it seems absolutely clear that headache sufferers do tend to be rather obsessional – and, therefore, exceptionally vulnerable to stress. This is not, of course, a criticism.

Obsessive people are invariably honest and extremely reliable and obsessiveness is a trait which benefits everyone apart from the victim him or herself. I mention this phenomenon because I think it may help some people.

If you are a regular headache or migraine sufferer answer these simple questions to find out whether you yourself are obsessional:

Do you invariably arrive at appointments early?

Do you always do what you promise to do?

Do you get cross with people who are unreliable?

Do people ever comment on the neatness of your handwriting?

Do you like to do the washing up and tidy up the house before you go to bed at night?

Do you always have a comb or hair brush handy so that you can keep your hair neat and tidy?

Do you get upset if people walk into your home wearing muddy shoes or boots?

Do you try to keep your car tidy?

Do you prefer formal gardens to natural, wild gardens?

Do you dislike having unexpected visitors?

If you answered 'yes' to more than two of these questions then you are basically an obsessional person.

You may be able to help cut down the number of headaches you suffer from by loosening up a little. You won't be able to stop being obsessive, of course. Obsessiveness is an inbuilt trait which cannot be entirely eradicated – you can't change that.

You may, however, be able to help yourself by making a genuine effort to learn how to relax your body and your mind, to get rid of the tensions which tend to accumulate as a result of your obsessive nature.

IRRITABLE BOWEL SYNDROME

Even knowing what damage stress can do doesn't make you immune. We are all potential victims.

For several months I had a persistent, nagging pain in my back. It was just about in the region of my right kidney. It didn't seem to be getting any worse but it certainly wasn't getting any better.

For a while I managed to convince myself that it was nothing more than a muscular backache caused by crouching over a typewriter. But then I noticed two additional symptoms.

I started feeling constantly 'full' – as though I had just eaten a large meal – and I found myself visiting the loo more often than I found entirely convenient. When I told my GP he took a routine urine sample, and found blood. The next step was a hospital appointment. Blood in the urine can be serious.

The ultrasound pictures showed a rather misshapen kidney. And more specialist X-ray pictures confirmed that there was something wrong. My kidney looked as though it was auditioning for a part as the hunchback of Notre Dame.

Unhappily, however, the radiologists couldn't get a really good view of my kidney. Their view was obscured by large bubbles of inconvenient gas lurking around in the coiled nooks and crannies of my intestinal loops. Extra help was needed.

HOW THE IRRITABLE BOWEL SYNDROME CAN BE CONTROLLED

ALTHOUGH WE KNOW A GOOD DEAL ABOUT THE CAUSES OF THE IRRITABLE BOWEL SYNDROME WE STILL DON'T KNOW HOW TO CURE IT. BUT, AS I HAVE LEARNED FIRST HAND, IT CAN BE CONTROLLED. OBVIOUSLY, SINCE STRESS IS A MAJOR CAUSE, LEARNING HOW TO CONTROL YOUR EXPOSURE TO STRESS – AND BUILD UP YOUR RESISTANCE TO IT – IS OF PRIMARY IMPORTANCE. AND I'LL SHOW YOU HOW TO DO THIS IN LATER CHAPTERS OF THIS BOOK.
BUT HERE ARE A FEW OF THE OTHER THINGS YOU CAN DO TO CONQUER THE SYNDROME:

- *FIRST, OF COURSE, YOU MUST **VISIT YOUR DOCTOR**. YOU SHOULD NEVER ASSUME THAT YOU HAVE IRRITABLE BOWEL SYNDROME UNTIL YOU HAVE SEEN YOUR DOCTOR AND DISCUSSED YOUR SYMPTOMS.*

- THERE ARE A NUMBER OF THINGS YOUR DOCTOR CAN DO TO HELP. HE MAY BE ABLE TO PRESCRIBE PILLS TO RELIEVE DIARRHOEA OR CONSTIPATION OR MAY RECOMMEND **PEPPERMINT OIL CAPSULES** FOR WIND.

- *YOU MAY FIND THAT GRADUALLY INCREASING **THE AMOUNT OF FLUID YOU DRINK** WILL HELP RELIEVE YOUR SYMPTOMS. AVOID DRINKING TOO MUCH MILK.*

- REDUCE YOUR **FAT INTAKE** BY CHOOSING LEAN CUTS IF YOU EAT MEAT.

- ***EAT MORE FIBRE.** SLOWLY BUILD UP YOUR CONSUMPTION OF FRESH VEGETABLES AND FRUIT, WHOLEMEAL BREAD OR HIGH BRAN CEREALS, WHOLEWHEAT PASTA AND BROWN RICE. (WARNING: YOU MAY SUFFER FROM INCREASED WIND IF YOU CHANGE YOUR DIET TOO QUICKLY.)*

- CUT DOWN YOUR **INTAKE OF MILK, CHEESE, BUTTER** AND OTHER DAIRY PRODUCTS, OR EVEN CUT THEM OUT COMPLETELY. TRY SKIMMED OR SEMI-SKIMMED MILK INSTEAD. AVOID BUTTER IN FAVOUR OF LOW FAT SPREADS.

- ***EXERCISE MORE.** WALK, SWIM, DANCE, CYCLE OR WORK OUT IN THE GYM. ALL THOSE THINGS WILL HELP YOU.*

- **KEEP WARM.** IF YOU ARE IN PAIN OR DISCOMFORT A WARM BATH MAY GIVE SOME RELIEF OR TRY A HOT WATER BOTTLE WRAPPED IN A TOWEL AND PRESSED AGAINST A PAINFUL TUMMY

So I was given an appointment to go to another, larger, city hospital for even more sophisticated tests. It was all very worrying. I knew that the doctors who had examined me suspected the worst. And without anyone saying anything I knew exactly how bad the worst could be. Very bad.

I breathed a huge sigh of relief when the kindly radiologist at the large city hospital told me that there was nothing seriously wrong with my kidney. It was, he assured me, misshapen but perfectly healthy.

And so, after racing up to Bristol to record a couple of TV programmes, and hurtling back home to write a newspaper column, I set off, as I had previously planned, to Paris.

On the plane flying over the Channel the pain in my back got much, much worse, and I suddenly realized what was wrong.

The gas that the radiologist had spotted in my intestines had expanded because of the change in air pressure and it was the gas that was causing my pain. It was the gas that was making me feel 'full' all the time, irritating my bowel and my bladder, and pressing on my kidney and causing the bleeding.

There was only one explanation for this apparently bizarre set of circumstances. Like millions of others, I had irritable bowel syndrome.

The moment I made the diagnosis I realized just *why* I had acquired this most common of 20th century disorders. There were two reasons.

First, I had been putting myself under an enormous amount of stress. For years I had run a series of passionate campaigns designed to spread the truth and oppose those parts of the medical establishment with which I disagreed. I had, for years, been spending at least 12 hours a day on my campaigns.

Second, I had changed my diet. I had cut out meat and fish and had dramatically increased the quantity of vegetables and cereals I was eating.

Although the irritable bowel syndrome has received little publicity or attention from the medical profession in recent years, I have little doubt that it is now one of the commonest of modern diseases. It is important to remember that although the irritable bowel syndrome is usually thought to affect young women it can (and does) affect men and people of all ages. It is probably as

THE SYMPTOMS AND CAUSES

FOR THE VAST MAJORITY OF SUFFERERS THERE ARE THREE BASIC SYMPTOMS:

- PAIN – USUALLY COLICKY AND SPASMODIC
- DIARRHOEA OR CONSTIPATION
- WIND

BUT THOSE ARE BY NO MEANS THE ONLY SYMPTOMS. SUFFERERS ALSO COMMONLY COMPLAIN OF:

- CONSTANTLY FEELING FULL
- NAUSEA, HEARTBURN OR INDIGESTION
- URINARY FREQUENCY
- BACKACHE
- TIREDNESS
- ANXIETY AND DEPRESSION

YOU MUST VISIT YOUR DOCTOR FOR A PRECISE DIAGNOSIS IF YOU THINK YOU COULD HAVE THE IRRITABLE BOWEL SYNDROME – OR IF YOU HAVE ANY OF THESE SYMPTOMS.

common as tooth decay and the common cold and more common than disorders such as diabetes.

There is little doubt that diet can play a part in the development of irritable bowel syndrome and some experts firmly believe that the modern, bland diet that most of us eat is at least partly responsible for the increase in this disorder, but there is also no doubt that the main cause is stress. We have known for years that tension and anxiety can have a tremendous influence on muscles, and it seems likely that stress and anxiety result in a tightening of the bowel muscles.

CANCER

Doctors have recognized for years that stress can cause a vast array of common diseases – including stomach ulcers, heart disease, high blood pressure, asthma, migraine and skin disease, but there is evidence to show that stress can cause cancer too.

It has been known for centuries that women who are depressed or unhappy are more likely to get cancer. Way back in the 2nd century a Roman doctor called Galen noticed this link.

During recent years, however, a growing number of doctors have come to recognize that it is the increase in the amount of stress which most of us are under these days, which explains why cancer – once a relatively rare disorder – has become one of our two biggest killers. (The other big killer – heart disease – is also stress related.)

Some people seem destined to develop stress-induced cancer because of their personalities. People who develop cancer often have had very unhappy childhoods, may have suffered a lot from loneliness when they were young, don't get enough love, or are very unselfish and spend a lot of time and energy trying to please other people.

People like this often feel a need to put a lot into their relationships with other people and to throw themselves into relationships wholeheartedly; they desperately need to be loved and when something goes wrong with their world, their bodies become weak and vulnerable to cancer.

It is the cells of the body's immune system which help to make sure that cancer cells do not grow.

Stress, especially the sort of deep-seated stress that can be created by a failing relationship, damages the efficiency of the immune cells which help to protect us against cancer, and numerous medical teams have shown that cancer is one of the disorders to which stress victims are vulnerable.

All this may sound worrying. But although the evidence suggests that thousands of people develop cancer because of broken relationships and mental weaknesses, there is also evidence to show that it is possible to turn these links between the mind and the body around and to use the same pathways to help cure cancers which have developed.

It took several years for the majority of doctors to accept that stress can cause cancer. Hopefully, it will not take as long for doctors to understand that it is possible to conquer or control cancer by teaching patients how to relax, by making them happy and by replacing their fears and anxieties with happy, positive, constructive, and comforting thoughts.

One early scientific paper has already shown that patients with breast cancer which has spread around their bodies will, on average, live 18 months longer if they are encouraged to use their minds in a positive and constructive way.

The best hope for cancer therapy does not come from drugs or surgery or from any bizarre, expensive alternative remedy. It comes from teaching patients how to use the power of their minds to help themselves fight their diseases.

Since it is now clear that it is our minds which can kill us, it is appropriate that it is our minds which can help get us better again – and help us lead longer, healthier lives.

HOW YOUR BODY RESPONDS TO STRESS

Every second of every minute of every day of your life, your nervous system receives about a 100 million messages, travelling at about 675 mph. Those messages come from every part of your body.

Clearly the less important messages have to be ignored, or at least put on one side temporarily while the urgent problems are dealt with. And that is exactly what your brain does.

As you read this you are breathing but you are not aware that your lungs are functioning (though, of course, if anything goes wrong the information coming from your lungs will suddenly take priority); you are perhaps digesting a meal but, again, unless something is going wrong, you will not be aware of the digestive processes. If you are concentrating properly, your mind will be cutting out all sorts of extraneous information gathered by your special senses systems. You will, for example, be able to ignore the sounds of the clock ticking or the refrigerator humming.

Apart from messages provided by your five senses (hearing, sight, smell, taste and touch), there are impulses from numerous receptors hidden deep inside

YOUR BODY UNDER STRESS

THE BLOOD FLOW TO YOUR BRAIN INCREASES SO YOU CAN THINK AND REACT MORE QUICKLY. THE PITUITARY GLAND RELEASES A SPECIAL HORMONE TO TRIGGER THE RELEASE OF HORMONES WHICH HELP PREPARE YOUR BODY FOR EMERGENCY ACTION.

YOUR HEARING WILL BECOME MORE SENSITIVE. ANIMALS PRICK UP THEIR EARS BUT IN HUMANS THIS SIMPLE REFLEX HAS BEEN LOST.

YOUR BREATHING RATE WILL GO UP TO GET AS MUCH OXYGEN AS POSSIBLE INTO YOUR LUNGS, AND THEREFORE YOUR BLOODSTREAM.

BLOOD FLOW TO THE SKIN DECREASES SO THAT AN INJURY WILL RESULT IN MINIMAL BLOOD LOSS, AND SO THAT AS MUCH BLOOD AS POSSIBLE WILL BE AVAILABLE TO SUPPLY YOUR TWO MOST VITAL ORGANS – YOUR BRAIN AND YOUR HEART.

YOUR PUPILS DILATE AND YOUR RETINA WILL BECOME MORE SENSITIVE TO LIGHT SO THAT YOUR VISION BECOMES MORE ACUTE.

HAIRS STAND UP ON END IN A VAIN ATTEMPT TO MAKE YOU LOOK LARGER AND MORE FIERCESOME.

MUSCLES BECOME TENSE SO THAT YOU CAN FIGHT MORE EFFECTIVELY.

PRESSURE WILL GO UP TO PUSH BLOOD ROUND YOUR BODY FASTER THAN USUAL (SO THAT TISSUES CAN BE SUPPLIED WITH FRESH OXYGEN AND FOOD SPEEDILY WHILE WASTE PRODUCTS ARE TAKEN AWAY EQUALLY FAST).

ACID WILL POUR INTO YOUR STOMACH TO TURN FOOD INTO ENERGY AS QUICKLY AS POSSIBLE.

your body. There are viscero-receptors which tell you what your internal organs are doing at any particular time; chemo-receptors telling you what sort of chemical condition your blood is in, and proprioceptors telling you what your muscles and tendons are doing. In addition there are, of course, messages from higher brain centres. Anticipation, fear, memory, imagination and other types of thinking can all produce impulses which clamour for attention.

Any particular stimulus can produce an infinite variety of other stimuli. For example, there will, at the very least, be a psychological effect and a physiological result. The psychological result may produce other psychological feelings. The physiological result may produce psychological reactions of its own and vice versa. Let me explain.

Imagine you are shopping in town with a small child to look after – your son or daughter, your grandson or granddaughter, or the child of a friend or neighbour. You are looking in a shop window. Suddenly you hear a squeal of brakes as a car narrowly avoids running over the child who has wandered into the road. Try to imagine how you will feel.

You will feel a physiological reaction as you automatically feel anxious to help. Your body will prepare yourself to deal with an emergency. Your heart rate will go up and your muscles will tense so that you are better able to run forward and save the child's life.

At the same time you will feel guilty about neglecting the child and frightened for its safety as well as relieved and happy that it has not been injured.

All the distress and worry and muscle tension and the acid pouring into your stomach (to turn food into energy) provide so powerful an effect that you are convinced you are about to have a heart attack.

Those are just a few of the stimuli that will clamour for some sort of action. The result will probably be such total confusion that for a moment you just stand there on the pavement and do nothing – frozen by indecision. You may not even cry. Your only reaction may be an automatic, half stifled cry of despair.

Many of the messages which travel to your brain never produce any reaction at all. Reactions only occur when the intensity of a sensation is considerable; and the intensity of a sensation depends upon the frequency with which impulses are received. Identical stimuli of equal potency may, of course, produce different results in different people and in different circumstances. The effects any stimulus has depends upon the age, sex, experiences and genetic make-up of the individual concerned, as well as upon the intake of drugs, diet and alcohol and the general physical status. For example, in old age there is a loss of adaptability to stimuli. The old suffer more when confronted with some stimuli, but suffer less when confronted with others.

The fact that impulses are ignored does not mean that they stop coming. On the contrary they never stop coming whatever is happening. The central nervous system is kept permanently up to date with information from touch receptors, organs of taste, smell, sight and hearing and from special receptors in the internal organs, the blood vessels and the muscles.

YOUR BODY ON AUTOMATIC PILOT

Much of the information which your brain receives is processed without you ever being consciously aware of it having arrived. Numerous information-collecting agencies throughout your body keep your brain permanently supplied with up to date information on the temperature of the environment, the state of your body's water and oxygen supplies and the position and state of your muscles and joints.

Your body is like one of those dolls with the lead-filled bases which rock back into position when buffeted from side to side. Numerous automatic defence mechanisms and regulatory agencies are permanently available to protect you from potentially dangerous environmental variations and physical stresses. These in-built protective mechanisms are vitally important, for your body is a delicate and sensitive organism which operates effectively only when certain basic, internal conditions are met.

The importance and effectiveness of these defence mechanisms is well-illustrated by the fact that, although your body can only survive when the temperature of your blood and body remains well between 30 and 45 degrees centigrade, you can survive when the temperature in the environment is much hotter or much colder than this. Your body's warning system, defence mechanisms and protective equipment enable it to adapt to rapidly changing conditions. It is these defence mechanisms which enable the Eskimo to survive in his cold igloo, the African tribesman to survive in the bush and the Arab to stay alive in the heat of the desert.

Your body maintains its stable internal environment by modifying its physical structure to suit the external environment. For example, if you get stranded in the desert your surface blood vessels will dilate so that your skin turns bright pink. The superficial blood flow will enable your body to lose considerable quantities of heat. Even more heat will be lost by your body's cunning use of the fact that when water evaporates, heat is lost. Just as people in hot climates keep their butter cool by storing it in water filled porous pots, which allow water to evaporate, so the human body loses heat by sweating. When the sweat evaporates, heat is lost into the surrounding air. If you are sweating you will automatically produce less saliva. So your mouth will become dry. And you will become thirsty and drink. All this ensures that your body's attempts to keep its temperature down do not result in a dangerous loss of necessary fluids.

Your body has another technique available to help it to lose heat. When you breathe out, heat will be lost on your breath. This is why dogs pant on hot days. Humans do the same but less dramatically. Incidentally, your body will produce less heat when it is still and so the natural response of a human being who is hot is to lie still and do nothing.

When, on the other hand, your body is surrounded by cold air the surface blood vessels constrict, so reducing the flow of blood through your skin. The surface hairs on your body stand up in a vain attempt to keep a layer of warm air trapped next to your skin. (In practice, of course, our lack of body hair means that cold weather merely produces useless goose pimples.) You shiver because this involves your muscles in physical activity which produces heat; you may even automatically stamp your feet to produce more heat.

Blood is a vital body constituent. It carries oxygen from your lungs to your tissues and removes waste products. Without a steady flow of blood your body will die, so when blood is lost your body employs a number of techniques designed to ensure that the supply that is left is used properly – rather in the way that electricity producers try to ensure that vital services continue to get supplies in emergencies. It is your brain and your heart which must always continue to be supplied properly, and so, to ensure that this happens, your body reduces the size of the vessels supplying your muscles and skin. At the same time the size of the vessels supplying your brain and heart will be increased. In addition, fluid will flow out of your tissues into the blood to help keep the blood volume at a good level (the shortage of tissue fluid produces a feeling of thirst which automatically helps to restore the lost fluids) and if there is a leak in the system at any point an automatic clotting mechanism comes into operation after giving the local blood vessels a chance to wash out any invading germs.

In addition to these mechanisms, which are designed to help maintain your body's status quo despite changes in the general environment, there are a number of automatic responses which will help to protect your body from a wide range of more specific potential hazards.

If someone mischievously tickles the end of your nose with a feather, you will probably sneeze because of a reflex designed to help you expel foreign bodies from inside your nostrils. If a foreign body gets down into your throat, you will cough and at the same time you will automatically swallow so that anything coughed up can be swept down your oesophagus and into your stomach. If the object is too big to be swallowed you will gag and the object will come flying out again; if it is poisonous then your stomach will probably reject it and you will be sick. If you put something into your mouth which is an irritant, the saliva will pour out of your salivary glands. If you walk into a sandstorm your eyelids will automatically close to protect your eyes, and the tears will flow to wash out your eyes and keep

"Your body's warning system, defence mechanisms and protective equipment enable it to adapt to rapidly changing conditions"

your conjunctiva clean. Sit on a nail and you will jump up because the sensation of pain automatically takes you away from the stimulus. Swallow threatening bacteria and you will develop vomiting and diarrhoea as your body tries to expel the unwanted and potentially dangerous invaders. Contract an infectious disease and your body temperature will rise to try and kill off the causative organisms. After heavy exercise, when you have used up stocks of sugar you will feel hungry. Your empty stomach will contract and go into spasm-producing hunger pangs which will be relieved by eating.

All these accurate, automatic responses show that your body invariably knows best. Unhappily, we rarely appreciate the efforts that our bodies make on our behalf. We damage our ability to respond to environmental changes by allowing our protective mechanisms to atrophy and by deliberately overriding them in the same way that office workers sometimes wedge open fire doors because it is more convenient. When we have an attack of bacteria-induced diarrhoea we take medicines to stop it. When we feel full we eat more. When we feel hot, instead of allowing our bodies to look after the problem for us, we impatiently eat ice cream and install air conditioning. We use powders to stop us sweating when we are hot. When our tonsils do the job for which they are intended and grow larger, we have them removed.

As a result of our cunning we develop many new and more disturbing disorders. We get colds and our infections last longer.

YOUR BODY
IN A STATE OF ALERT

Some information requires immediate attention which your body's automatic defence mechanisms cannot cope with alone. If, for example, you are standing in a quiet room where you think you are alone and a cat knocks a plate onto the floor behind you, your body is immediately prepared for a crisis. It could be a burglar.

In order to enable you to find out more about the potential crisis, and to help you decide just how important it is, there will be an immediate increase in the sensitivity of the sense organs:

Here is another immediate reaction which isn't visible.

Your pituitary gland will release something called

- **YOUR PUPILS WILL DILATE AND YOUR RETINA WILL BECOME MORE SENSITIVE TO LIGHT SO THAT VISION BECOMES MORE ACUTE.**

- **YOUR HEARING WILL ALSO BECOME MORE SENSITIVE. ANIMALS PRICK UP THEIR EARS BUT IN HUMANS THIS REFLEX HAS LONG BEEN LOST.**

- **YOUR HEAD WILL AUTOMATICALLY TURN TOWARDS THE STIMULUS SO THAT THE BEST POSSIBLE INFORMATION CAN BE OBTAINED.**

- **YOUR MUSCLES WILL TENSE, READY FOR ACTION, AND YOUR HEART BEAT WILL SLOW TEMPORARILY.**

- **BLOOD FLOW TO YOUR BRAIN WILL INCREASE SO THAT THE BEST POSSIBLE USE OF AVAILABLE BRAIN TISSUE CAN BE MADE.**

- **BLOOD FLOW TO YOUR LIMBS WILL DIMINISH SO THAT IF YOUR LIMBS ARE INJURED THE AMOUNT OF BLOOD LOST WILL BE MINIMIZED.**

an adrenocorticotrophic hormone which will stimulate your adrenal gland to produce steroids and adrenalin – hormones which increase your blood pressure, close down your superficial blood vessels and improve the blood supply to your muscles. The shrinking of the surface blood vessels ensures that, if your body is damaged, you will lose as little blood as possible while, at the same time, the blood supply to your essential organs and muscles will be maintained.

Acid will flow into your stomach to ensure that any food there is turned into sugar as quickly as possible. Your muscles will be tensed ready for action. (A less useful reaction is the erection of the body hairs. When a cat is frightened, its hairs stand on end, making it look larger and more fearsome. When a human being is frightened, the same thing happens but unfortunately human body hairs are too short to make any noticeable difference in the apparent size of the owner. The reaction is automatic but useless.)

As a result of all these changes you will be able to defend yourself much better. You will – if necessary – be able to run faster, jump higher and hit harder than you would have thought possible – and you will be able to act far more quickly too.

WHEN IT IS A FALSE ALARM

If it becomes clear that the danger has been exaggerated, then your adrenal glands will shut down and your body's response will stop. However, your body's adaptability has strictly finite limits. If the stimuli still persist your body will react again.

This mechanism of adaptation can be explained with a simple example.

If you are sitting in a room with a clock ticking, your awareness of the ticking will slowly fade as your body gets used to it; the receptors which pick up the impulses transmitted from your ears become disinterested in the information. There is no need to act upon it and so, although the stimulus doesn't go away, your body ignores it. (However, if the clock stops ticking or ticks a little louder, you will become aware of it again. The stimulus will have changed and so the receptors will have to pass on this new information so that your brain can decide whether or not it is important.)

Although your body can adapt, its ability to ignore information is limited. A clock which ticks very loudly and persistently may be ignored for a while, but it will eventually force the fact of its presence back into your consciousness. You will hear the ticking again. And once your body's adaptive mechanisms have failed you will continue to be aware of the ticking. Eventually, you may find the ticking quite unbearable.

THE INTERNAL THREAT

In other animals, a stimulus from the outside world is necessary before the system described can be activated. But in human beings there is not necessarily a need for an outside stimulus. The impulse can come from brain centres rather than the external environment.

Such vague and introspective processes as thought and anticipation can trigger a response. Problems then often arise because your body cannot differentiate between physical and intellectual anxieties.

If you are faced with an armed burglar you must kill him, escape or be killed and your body will respond in a predetermined way to help you act effectively. But if you lose your job, your body will respond in an identical, but wholly inappropriate, way.

In both situations there will be changes in your heart rate and blood pressure and so on.

The difference is that whereas the confrontation with the burglar will probably end fairly quickly, your joblessness may last for a long time and consequently the effects are likely to persist.

The result is that the man who loses his job is likely to get persistent high blood pressure, have a heart attack or develop a stomach ulcer as a permanent reminder of his problem.

The unemployed man may want to find a job and may look hard for a job but he does not have control over his destiny and his body's physical attempts to help him are worse than useless – they are positively harmful. His body continues to try and help him cope, under the mistaken impression that the crisis state requires immediate action and unaware that the help is unwanted. His blood pressure will stay high, acid will continue to pour into the stomach and his muscles will stay tight and tense.

The human body is designed for operation in environments where action must be taken quickly in response to stressful stimuli and where stimuli encountered are unlikely to persist. As the pace of modern life increases, so the number of impulses likely to incite a response from the body also increases.

We live in stressful times not because stress-inducing events are by themselves any more traumatic than the events of a century ago, but simply because there are likely to be more of them and because there is less opportunity to escape from them.

There are, as I have already explained, many people whose job it is deliberately to increase the amount of stress we are under. Sadly, the continued and continuing physiological changes inspired by persistent problems result in enormous amounts of damage being done to our bodies.

CHAPTER THREE

Identifying The Forces Which Drive You

Most of have very little real control over our lives. We don't usually do things because we *really* want to do them. We do them because we know that we're expected to do them, because we know that other people want us to do them and because we are obeying hidden driving forces of which we may well be largely unaware.

Personal, internal influences such as ambition, vanity and lust all push us into doing things that we might not otherwise choose to do.

> *"We don't usually do things because we really want to do them. We do them because we know that we're expected to do them"*

Imagine it is Saturday night and the lights are still burning in the offices of The Inter Galactic Plastic Grommet and Blue Paper Rivet Company. Several people are still at work preparing a marketing strategy for a new type of transparent, heat-resistant, red paper rivet. Let's look at why each of these people is working so late.

John is 62 years old and the Chairman and Managing Director of The Inter Galactic Plastic Grommet and Blue Paper Rivet Company. He built up the company from scratch and still owns 51 per cent of the shares, but his main driving force is a determination to hand over a large, thriving business to his grandson. John's big disappointment in life is that he has no son of his own. His only daughter married a doctor who has no interest in working for the company. But he does have a nine-year-old grandson on whom he dotes. John wants to start a dynasty of his own – something that will last for ever – and the company is his path to immortality. His primary driving force tonight is **ambition**.

Neil is 58 years old. He has worked for John Roberts all his life. He is now the Company Secretary. He respects and admires his boss enormously and would do anything for him. He is at the meeting because he doesn't entirely trust some of the younger executives in the company.

He suspects that some of them are more interested in their own careers than in the success of the new rivet, and he wants to help look after the company's interests. His primary driving force tonight is **loyalty**.

Mary is John's personal assistant. She is 27 years old and married, but her marriage is an unhappy one. Her husband drinks too much and she knows that he will be out drinking with his friends tonight. She has no children. Mary doesn't claim any overtime for working late but stays at the office because she doesn't want to go home and sit alone in front of the television set. Her primary driving force tonight is **boredom**.

Michael is an executive in the company. He is 32 years old and married with two children, but he is desperately in love with Mary. He doesn't really need to be at the meeting – he is the Production Manager – but is there because it is an excuse to be with Mary. His primary driving force tonight is **lust**.

Peter, the Marketing Manager, is 43 years old and really wanted to be at home. It is his wedding anniversary and his wife had arranged a celebratory dinner party. But Peter has two children at college, a large mortgage and an overdraft. He knows that he is probably too old to find another job at the same salary, so he is at the meeting because he is too frightened not to be there. His primary driving force tonight is **fear**.

Jane, the Public Relations Director, is 33 years old, unmarried and intensely proud of her status within the company. She is far more interested in what goes on within the company than outside it. Most of the executives have the title 'manager' but Jane has persuaded John to make her a director of the company. She has a bigger and more expensive car than all the other executives and, apart from John, has the biggest and most lavishly equipped office in the building. She has her own car parking space and her secretary has the title 'Executive Assistant'. She fought for three months to have her own executive washroom built in a corner of her office. Jane is at the meeting because she is terrified of something happening behind her back that might adversely affect her status within the company. Her primary driving force tonight is **vanity**.

Jim, 28, designed the new rivet. He is married with two small children. He is very proud of his rivet-designing skills and he thinks that this latest rivet is the best thing he has ever done. He is at the meeting because he doesn't want the others to 'mess up' the marketing of what he thinks of as his 'baby'. His primary driving force tonight is **pride**.

Doreen, 44, is the Sales Manager. She has two teenage daughters who are away at boarding school, is divorced and for three months has been living with a waiter who is 22 years her junior. She is consumed by guilt – an emotion which governs her life. She feels guilty about the break-up of her marriage (she was having an affair with one of the salesmen who works for her); she feels guilty about sending her daughters away to boarding school (she hardly ever sees them any more and seems to have nothing in common with them); she feels guilty about the fact that she lives with someone so much younger than herself and she feels guilty about the fact that, when her mother died recently, she was at an industrial fair in Chicago selling rivets and couldn't get home in time. Most relevant of all, however, she feels guilty about the fact that a month ago she lost an important order for the company when she was rude to an important client. No one else knows that it was her fault that the order was lost. Doreen blamed a junior salesman whom she subsequently fired. (She feels guilty about that too.) Doreen doesn't really need to be at this meeting. But she is there because she feels that she has let the company down. Many driving forces are straightforward and easy to understand. But guilt, the most subtle and most destructive of all driving forces is different. (See box on page 38.) Doreen's primary driving force tonight is **guilt**.

GUILT –
THE MOST IMPORTANT
DRIVING FORCE OF ALL

Guilt is a driving force that is as common as love and as damaging as hate. It is more insidious, more difficult to escape and more persistently destructive than lust, ambition or vanity.

Most of us suffer from it some of the time, some of us suffer from it all of the time. The more you care about others and the more sensitive and considerate you are, the more you will be likely to suffer.

Fanatics don't know what guilt is because they are so filled with a feeling of self-righteous indignation that there is no room for any self-doubt. Because they are driven by some force that seems greater and more powerful than anything else, they never worry about what other people think. The single, driving obsession that fires the fanatic leaves no room for such expressions of sensitivity as regret and shame – the basic materials from which the rest of us create our own guilt.

Psychopaths remain free of guilt because they are entirely devoid of the sort of feelings that the rest of us describe as love and compassion. Since those are the emotions which lead directly to guilt the psychopath is immune; without *caring* it is impossible to feel guilty.

We tend to think of guilt in cold, black and white terms. We know that we feel guilty when we do something that we know is wrong. The simplest type of guilt is the sort we get when we have broken a window, taken something without paying or broken a law.

But most guilt is not like that. Most really damaging and destructive guilty feelings are not inspired by any great crime – or even by a small crime for that matter – but by subtle and destructive feelings of self-criticism and by towering feelings of inadequacy – often inspired by our inevitable inability to match the impossible expectations of those whom we hold in greatest awe.

Much of our guilt is inspired by the (conscious or unconscious) manipulations of those who we respect and love most. Those who love the most – and have the greatest feelings for the people around them – are the most likely to suffer from guilt.

Guilt is difficult to define, but in practical terms most of us find it hard to distinguish the pain, and the anguish it inspires, from the agonies we associate with what we commonly call our 'conscience'; the indefinable internal self-regulatory mechanism with which we punish ourselves when we have done something wrong But there are differences between the two.

Conscience is a clearly defined dividing line which separates good from evil and bad from good. There can never be very much doubt about whether something

"Those who love the most - and have the greatest feelings for the people around them - are the most likely to suffer from guilt"

falls into the good category or the bad category.

But the feeling of guilt we suffer when we suspect that we may have done wrong (or, most commonly, failed to do right) is an entirely internal phenomenon. It is something that we do to ourselves because we feel that we have failed. We may have failed to do something we feel we should have done. Or we may have done something that we feel we should not have done. Either way, the result is the same; we torture ourselves with self-recrimination. Having prosecuted ourselves we find ourselves guilty. Guilt is one of the most powerful and damaging of human emotions and, ironically, it is an emotion that is soundly and exclusively built on love and compassion and respect.

There are so many possible sources of guilt that it is quite impossible to classify them all. But most types of guilt fall into one of two main categories.

On the one hand there are the varieties of guilt that result from our personal relationships with other people. These are probably the most damaging of all because they are inspired by people whose opinions and feelings we respect most highly. (See box on page 38.)

On the other hand, there are the types of guilt which are created by society; or, to be more precise, by the demands, teachings and expectations of those around us. Most of us have an inbuilt sense of right and wrong and if we trespass against it, we feel guilty. This sense of right and wrong does not come, however, from some mysterious, inherited force and is not universal or God given – it is not the same as a conscience. It comes instead from religious and social prejudices which have been created, established and nurtured by example and instruction. Some of these forces seem sound, simple and logical, but others are less easy to explain.

Most of us feel guilty if we steal because stealing is considered to be an antisocial activity that is wrong.

Other feelings of guilt are more difficult to explain though since they develop from prejudices and fears which do not have any easily sustainable origins.

Many of us feel guilty if we lie in bed on Saturday or Sunday mornings, if we acquire money too easily, if we allow ourselves to be seen naked in public or if we sit down in the cinema in the afternoon when we feel we should be at work.

These types of guilt are created by social mores which have been established by a huge variety of religious leaders, politicians and teachers. All this guilt has a number of damaging effects on the way we live but the greatest and most destructive effect is to make us feel inferior and inadequate and to damage our self-confidence and self esteem.

When we feel guilty because we have failed to live up to the expectations of those around us – be they relatives, friends or teachers – we feel insecure and we lose our confidence. The extent of our love or respect for the people we think we have failed will determine the extent of guilt. For most of us, our sense of shame and loss of self-esteem is most easily related to our feelings for our parents. When we feel that we have let them down, we punish ourselves with exceptional and unforgiving severity.

The type of internal pressure produced by feelings of guilt is the most damaging type of all varieties of stress because it is so impossible to escape and because the consequences can be so far-reaching. Many workaholics – who cannot relax but who must constantly force themselves to work harder and harder – are driven by a lack of self-esteem and a burning fear of failure. Many individuals who push themselves too hard – however great their achievements may be – do so because of a continuing and inescapable sense of inadequacy, probably inspired by a continuing urge to elicit praise from their parents. Guilt is a major cause of heart disease, irritable bowel syndrome, headaches and a hundred and one other stress-related disorders.

DON'T WORRY ABOUT ME!

In the box on the right are some guilt-inducing phrases that we have all heard, and probably used, many times – usually to people we care about very much. Most of the time people say these things without realizing just how much they are manipulating the ones they love. But sometimes people deliberately use phrases like these to get their own way.

PHRASES THAT CREATE GUILT

- 'DON'T WORRY ABOUT ME – I'LL BE ALL RIGHT'

- 'YOU WOULDN'T DO THAT IF YOU LOVED ME'

- 'I'LL STAY IN BY THE PHONE JUST IN CASE YOU RING'

- 'I SPENT CHRISTMAS ALONE THINKING OF YOU'

- 'YOU'LL NEVER KNOW THE SACRIFICES WE MADE FOR YOU'

- 'I'M DOING THIS FOR YOU'

- 'SEND ME A CARD IF YOU HAVE A MOMENT TO THINK ABOUT ME'

KNOW YOUR DRIVING FORCES

TRADITIONALLY, INFLUENCES AFFECTING HUMAN BEHAVIOUR DIVIDE INTO SEVEN VIRTUES:

- PRUDENCE • TEMPERANCE
- FORTITUDE • JUSTICE
- FAITH • HOPE
- LOVE

AND SEVEN SINS:

- PRIDE
- COVETOUSNESS
- LUST
- ENVY
- GLUTTONY
- ANGER
- SLOTH

But these 14 qualities are sadly inadequate when it comes to classifying human actions.

Who would deny that inferiority, loyalty and boredom are important driving forces which influence what we do – and why and when we do it? And what about guilt, perhaps the most important force of all?

Within each one of us there are numerous driving forces derived from genetic and environmental influences which affect the ways in which we act.

There is, for example, always some selfish self-satisfying motive for any action. It may sound cold-blooded but relationships succeed when both parties gain something and, generally speaking, most people behave in order to satisfy themselves.

Though we may resist the idea, the inescapable truth is that when one person helps another, the subject is the beneficiary just as often as the recipient. The voluntary worker who spends several hours every week helping the elderly, the sick and the infirm is satisfying his or her own urges and needs. All good deeds are basically selfish – though this does not in any way detract from their value.

In each relationship and each situation there will be a number of primary driving forces.

If your car is stolen, you will probably be angry with the thief, feel guilty about having forgotten to lock the car door and anxious about whether or not your insurance company will pay up.

If you have been sacked, you will probably be angry with your employer, depressed about your failure to hold your job and concerned and anxious about those who depend upon you.

In any situation, the action you take will result directly from the combination of driving forces which result from your emotional responses.

If you understand the driving forces which push you into behaving the way you do then you will find it much easier to come to terms with your own weaknesses, to influence fate, to anticipate and avoid problems, to improve the quality of your relationships with other people and to control the stress in your life.

Look at the two lists on the right and overleaf. The list includes just a few of the things that you may have done during the last month and that could have worried you or increased the stress in your life. The second includes some reasons why you may have done them – the primary driving forces which control your life.

Try to decide which driving force has pushed you hardest in each situation. By defining and understanding the reasons why you do things you will find it much easier to control your life. Most of us have remarkably little control over our own lives. We work hard at jobs we don't like so that we can earn money to spend on things we don't really need. We create our own stresses. By understanding how those stresses develop you can learn how to conquer them.

ACTIONS

HOW MANY OF THESE THINGS HAVE YOU DONE IN THE LAST MONTH?

- BEEN NICE TO SOMEONE YOU DON'T LIKE

- *BEEN NASTY TO SOMEONE YOU LIKE OR LOVE*

- ATTENDED A DINNER PARTY THAT YOU DIDN'T WANT TO GO TO AND DIDN'T ENJOY

- *ATTENDED A MEETING THAT YOU DIDN'T ENJOY OR GET ANYTHING OUT OF*

- LIED TO PROTECT SOMEONE YOU LOVE OR LIKE

- *LIED TO PROTECT SOMEONE YOU DISLIKE*

- WRITTEN SOMETHING THAT YOU LATER REGRETTED

- *SAID SOMETHING UNPLEASANT ABOUT SOMEONE YOU LIKE*

- AGREED TO DO SOMETHING THAT YOU DON'T WANT TO DO

DRIVING FORCES

NOW TRY TO DECIDE WHY YOU DID WHAT YOU DID! THIS LIST DOES NOT INCLUDE SIMPLE REASONS LIKE 'ANGER'. IT IS THE UNDERLYING REASON BEHIND YOUR ANGER THAT IS MORE IMPORTANT.

- AMBITION
- ANXIETY
- BITTERNESS
- BOREDOM
- CONFORMITY
- COVETOUSNESS
- COWARDICE
- ENVY
- EXCITEMENT
- FAITH
- FEAR
- GREED
- GUILT
- HATE
- HOPE
- JEALOUSY
- KINDNESS AND SOFT HEARTEDNESS
- LOVE
- LOYALTY
- LUST
- MASOCHISM
- OBSTINENCE
- PITY
- PREJUDICE
- PRESTIGE
- PRIDE
- RESPECT
- RESPONSIBILITY
- SADISM
- SELFISHNESS
- SHYNESS
- SLOTH
- STUBBORNNESS
- VANITY

IS WORK WRECKING YOUR HEALTH?

Workaholism – an unhealthy inability to stop working – is becoming more and more common. It is often caused by a long-standing feeling of inadequacy. Some workaholics push themselves too hard because they are frightened of something: usually failure or poverty. Many simply feel the need to prove themselves better than anyone else.

If work is ruining your health it isn't too late to protect yourself. First ask yourself these simple questions:

1. Are you always busy?
2. Do you feel constantly under pressure?
3. Do you wish you had more time for yourself?
4. Do you find it difficult to relax?
5. Are you unwilling to take a holiday – even though you need one?
6. Do you have difficulty in sleeping?
7. Do you work at evenings and weekends?
8. Do you snatch meals while you work?
9. Do you ever wake up at night thinking about work or money?
10. Do you find it difficult to slow down your mind ?

If you have answered 'yes' to any of these questions then you are almost certainly a workaholic.
Here are some of the diseases you could suffer from:

- **Eczema or dermatitis**
- **Indigestion**
- **Irritable Bowel Syndrome**
- **Arthritis**
- **High blood pressure**
- **Asthma**
- **Headaches or migraines**

You don't have to fit into a particular working category to be a workaholic.

People working for themselves often become victims as they struggle to create a successful business and employees can also be victims – particularly if they are working in a tough, competitive environment with a ruthless and domineering boss. Housewives, too, are as likely to suffer as anyone. The result will be more and more ill health.

But you can help yourself survive – in good health – by following some simple rules:

1. Cut out unnecessary work whenever possible. This is just as important at home as at work. Many chores become habits – even though they may not be necessary. Don't wash the car unless it's really dirty. Never iron socks or knickers.

2. Always leave a quarter of your time unscheduled. If you pack your day with appointments and commitments then the inevitable crises will throw you into a panic.

3. Make a list of everything you've got to do each week. Put urgent items on one list; less urgent items on a second list and non-urgent items on a third list. This way you can make sure that you do the urgent stuff first – before you get chased.

4. Break down big jobs into small, manageable parts to reduce the stress levels.

5. If you have to take on something new, try and make sure that you give up something that you are already doing – otherwise your work quota will simply expand until you collapse.

6. Allow other people to help you as often as possible. At work, delegate whenever you can. Try to surround yourself with people who you can trust. At home, when they are old enough, get the kids to help with the washing up and peel the potatoes; then, gradually increase their responsibilities.

7. Make relaxation a priority – and put it onto your 'urgent' list every week. You should spend some time every day relaxing – and you need to be able to relax effectively and thoroughly.

8. Make physical fitness a priority – put visits to the gym on your 'urgent' list too. The fitter you are, the better you will be able to cope with stress and pressure.

9. Don't let your work invade every aspect of your life. If you take work home, make sure that you only work in one room.

10. Learn to say 'no'. It may be hard. But it is often a lot easier than saying 'yes' to things that you don't really want to do, and for which you haven't time.

Finally, don't make the mistake of thinking that you are indispensable. Graveyards are full of people who thought they were indispensable.

IF YOU WANT TO KNOW JUST HOW INDISPENSABLE YOU ARE TRY THIS:

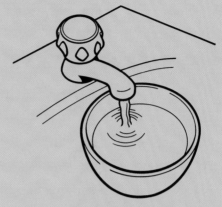

• FILL A BOWL WITH WARM WATER

• PUT YOUR HAND INTO THE BOWL

• TAKE YOUR HAND OUT

LOOK AT THE SIZE OF THE HOLE YOUR HAND LEAVES WHEN YOU REMOVE IT - *THAT'S* HOW INDISPENSABLE YOU ARE!

CHAPTER FOUR

Understanding The Forces Which Drive You

There are only two ways to ensure that stress does not ruin your health and your life: you can reduce the amount of stress in your life or you can improve your ability to cope with stress.

Some stresses are unavoidable. It is simply impossible to stay alive these days without being surrounded by stresses. Much that we do is potentially stressful. And much of the time the stress you encounter will be outside your influence. There just isn't anything you can do to banish the sort of potential stresses that are produced by advertisers and politicians and others who want you to behave in a particular way or who want you to spend your money on a special product. Those stresses – the ones that I call toxic stresses – will be there whatever you do. But that does not mean that those stresses are impossible to avoid or impossible to escape from.

"There are many ways in which you can minimize the effect of toxic stress on your life and there are, without doubt, many stresses in your life you can avoid"

There are many ways in which you can minimize the effect of toxic stress on your life and there are, without doubt, many stresses in your life that you can avoid.

To start with, make a list of all the things that put you under pressure at work, at home, in the daytime, in the evenings and at weekends. If you attend meetings that you find stressful or a nuisance, put them down. If you play sports that you take very seriously, put them down too. Many people think they are escaping from stress by playing tennis, squash, football or badminton or by going jogging or by spending time in the gym. They may well be helping themselves – as I will show later exercise can be very relaxing – but it is perfectly possible to increase your stress load to damaging and unbearable levels if you take your sport too seriously.

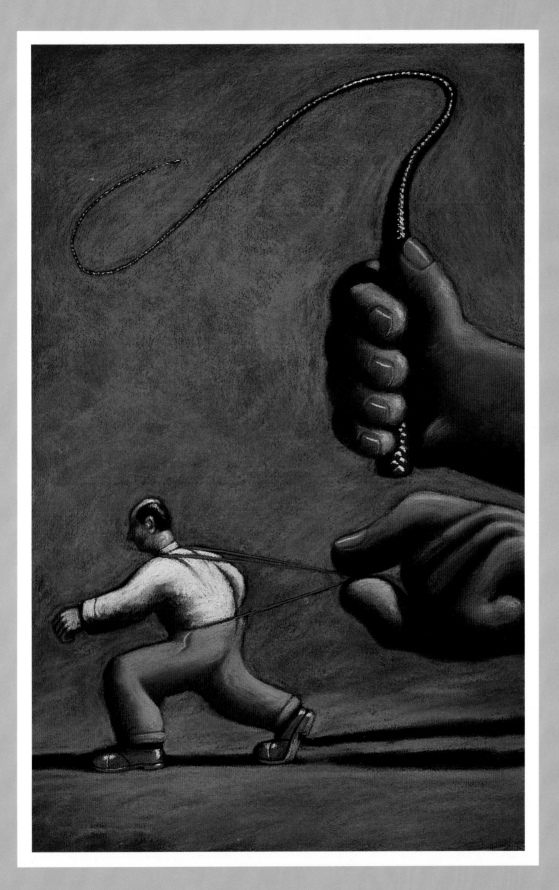

YOUR PERSONAL STRESS AND PRIORITY CHART

MAKE A LIST OF EVERYTHING THAT YOU DO:
JOBS, HOBBIES, SPORTS, OUTSIDE RESPONSIBILITIES (COMMITTEES, VOLUNTARY WORK).

LOOK AT EACH ACTIVITY OR RESPONSIBILITY CRITICALLY, THEN GIVE EACH ONE A PERSONAL PRIORITY rating of **1** TO **10** (P).

NEXT DECIDE HOW IMPORTANT EACH ACTIVITY IS TO OTHER PEOPLE IN YOUR LIFE – BUT ONLY THE PEOPLE WHO MATTER. GIVE IT A FAMILY PRIORITY RATING OF **1** TO **10** (F).

FINALLY, DECIDE HOW STRESSFUL EACH PARTICULAR ACTIVITY IS – AND GIVE IT A STRESS LEVEL rating of **1** TO **10** (S).

SO, FOR EXAMPLE, IF YOU ARE ON THE PARENT TEACHERS ASSOCIATION COMMITTEE YOU MAY CHOOSE TO GIVE IT A PERSONAL PRIORITY OF 1, A FAMILY PRIORITY OF 7 AND A STRESS LEVEL OF 10. ON THE OTHER HAND YOUR WEEKLY GAME OF TENNIS OR GOLF MAY HAVE A PERSONAL PRIORITY OF 10, A FAMILY PRIORITY OF 1 AND A STRESS LEVEL OF 0.

ONCE YOU HAVE FINISHED YOUR LIST GO THROUGH IT CRITICALLY. FOR EACH ACTIVITY ADD TOGETHER THE TWO PRIORITY SCORES (P+F). IF THE TOTAL DOES NOT EXCEED THE STRESS SCORE (S) THEN THE ACTIVITY IS DOING YOU - AND YOUR FAMILY - MORE HARM THAN GOOD AND SHOULD HAVE A LOW PRIORITY IN YOUR LIFE. IF THE TOTAL OF THE TWO PRIORITY SCORES (P+F) EXCEEDS THE STRESS SCORE (S) THEN THE ACTIVITY SHOULD HAVE A HIGHER PRIORITY IN YOUR LIFE: THE MORE THE SUM OF P+F EXCEEDS THE S THE GREATER THE PRIORITY THAT ACTIVITY SHOULD HAVE.

So, now you can easily mark your priorities, and mark those stresses that you could avoid!

You will undoubtedly realize that there are many things on your list that are only there because you don't like to say 'no', and are worried about offending people and because you think you ought to do them.

Guilt is a great driving force and many people just like you, allow their lives to be controlled by what they feel other people will think about them. Try hard not to feel so guilty, try to think of yourself and your priorities a little more. Try and remember that if you push yourself too hard your health will suffer; and the people and causes which are most important to you will suffer.

Try to pluck up the courage to be a little more selfish, to stand up for yourself more, to decide how you are going to spend your time and what you are going to do with your life.

WHY PRIORITIES ARE IMPORTANT

Failure to differentiate between the really important things in your life – and the less important things – can lead to a stress overload and a variety of serious health problems.

Pressures, worries and problems of all sizes can all have an adverse effect on your body and your mind, and the smaller problems and the insignificant worries can have just as devastating an effect on your health as the major problems.

If you do not learn to distinguish between the important priorities in your life and the less important priorities, you will suffer in a number of ways.

The number of problems to which you are exposed will grow and grow and grow. If you allow yourself to worry about the scratch on your car and the insult from your boss, your mind will add these anxieties to the other, more essential worries that you have. Unless you make a conscious decision to separate minor problems from major problems your mind will treat them all in exactly the same way and while you are wasting valuable time on insignificant worries, you will be failing to deal with the important things in your life.

Your health, the health of those you love, and the success of the causes you support are the things in your life which deserve your closest attention.

TIPS FOR SURVIVAL

1. Whenever you are faced with a problem try to see it in perspective. Is a missing sock so important? Will a late train result in personal ruin? Is a leaking washing machine really the end of the world?

2. Try to plan your life and put your aims, ambitions and priorities into a 'lifeplan' where perspective is important. What do you want to be doing in five, ten or 15 years time? How do you want to spend the rest of your life? How many of the things that you worry about each day would you willingly spend time on if today was your last day on earth? How important will some of today's problems seem in six months' time or five years' time?

3. Decide how you can best achieve your aims, then tackle your problems one by one. If you worry about everything at once you will never get anywhere. Be realistic. You will be far more successful than you could have dared hope to be.

4. Don't be fooled into spending time or energy or money on products or ambitions that are not really important to you. If you buy a car you can't afford – simply so that you can impress strangers on the way to work – you will have to work night and day to earn the money to pay for the servicing and insurance. If you have a swimming pool built in the garden to impress the neighbours, you'll probably spend every pleasant summer evening fishing leaves and slugs out of it – and having to put up with the neighbour's noisy children. If you buy a country cottage because everyone else has one, you will probably spend every weekend worrying about gutters, blocked drains and the overgrown garden. You can protect yourself against these unnecessary stresses by sorting out your priorities beforehand.

5. Don't make unrealistic goals for yourself, or else you will increase your stress levels dramatically. Keep your big dreams by all means but don't expect miracles. If you expect too much of yourself too quickly then you will be for ever disappointed.

6. Ask yourself how many of the things you do are done to please other people – people who don't really matter to you! Your life should be planned around your needs and wants and the genuine wants and needs of those whom you love.

CHAPTER FIVE

How Much Is Stress Affecting Your Life?

Many doctors now agree that at least nine out of every ten symptoms and nine out of every ten illnesses are either directly caused by stress, or are made considerably worse by it. Stress is powerful and destructive and toxic stress is the commonest, most far-reaching and most destructive force at work in any modern society anywhere in the world today.

Like personal stresses, toxic stress can cause an enormous range of individual symptoms and well-defined diseases. It can cause headaches, skin rashes and bowel disorders. It can cause asthma, high blood pressure, heart disease and stomach ulceration. It can cause depression, psoriasis and sexual problems. It can cause sleeplessness, hair loss and backache. It can make existing diseases worse and it can increase your susceptibility to infectious diseases, psychological problems and cancer.

"Stress is powerful and destructive and toxic stress is the commonest, most far-reaching and most destructive force at work in any modern society anywhere in the world today"

Sometimes stress also causes a type of exhaustion known as 'burn-out'. Burn-out is more than just tiredness. People who suffer from it lose their fight and their will to go on. They struggle through each day with no clear idea of what they are doing – or why.

My researches over the last 20 years have also convinced me that in addition to these well-recognized illnesses, toxic stress is also responsible for something else – something specific and something that has never before been recognized as an individual syndrome. I have named the disease caused by toxic stress 'The Twentieth Century Blues'.

The Twentieth Century Blues is one of the most common diseases in the developed world; as common as the common cold and far more damaging than any other common ailment.

The range of individuals suffering from this discomforting and incapacitating disorder is vast. The executive or company director who works for a large company, and who seems, on the surface, to have more control over his environment than his employees do, is as vulnerable to the effects of toxic stress as anyone else. The housewife, the student, and the nurse are all potential victims. The retired bank manager is just as vulnerable as the young bank clerk and the shop assistant is as likely to suffer as the chairman of the store.

The only common factor is that victims of The Twentieth Century Blues tend to be sensitive, and caring individuals. The more thoughtful and imaginative you are, the more you are likely to become a victim and the more likely you are to suffer.

The unintelligent and the uncaring are not, however, immune to the power of toxic stress. I believe that much modern hooliganism and vandalism is a result of toxic stress. The sensitive and intelligent respond to toxic stress by becoming unhappy and confused. The insensitive and unintelligent respond to toxic stress by becoming angry, aggressive and violent. The deep sense of frustration commonly felt by the victims of toxic stress can lead one individual to withdraw and become more alone. The same frustration can lead another, with a different personality and living in a different environment, to become a dangerous sociopath.

Why, if toxic stress and The Twentieth Century Blues are so common, have neither of them been recognized and written about by doctors before now?

Doctors are trained to look for physical causes and physical solutions to diseases. Ever since the modern medical profession developed in the mid 19th century, doctors have tried to find anatomical, physiological or biochemical explanations for all health problems.

It took years for doctors to accept that psychological pressures could cause any sort of illness and the general significance of stress was only recognized fairly recently by the profession as a whole.

It is not by accident that doctors are trained to try and cure illness by prescribing pills or intervening in some other essentially practical way. Doctors earn their living by providing practical services, and the links between the medical profession and the powerful drugs industry are extremely close.

Indeed, the sad truth is that, although doctors have not yet recognized the existence of toxic stress or The Twentieth Century Blues, they have for several years now been attempting to treat the symptoms suffered by people who are toxic stress victims. And their attempts to treat such patients – usually by prescribing tranquillizers or sleeping tablets have frequently made things worse rather than better. Tranquillizers, as I will show in the next chapter, solve none of the fears or anxieties caused by toxic stress, and cure none of the problems associated with The Twentieth Century Blues. Indeed, because they are frequently addictive, simply treating the symptoms not curing the causes, and have side effects, tranquillizers have created many new problems.

The simple fact is that medical treatment is not the answer to toxic stress or The Twentieth Century Blues, because neither toxic stress nor the syndrome it produces are essentially medical problems. The word 'toxic' is used as a synonym for 'poison' and toxic stress is an insidious, morally and spiritually, destructive disease. It eats away at the soul but it is not a disease that is ever likely to respond to a pharmacological therapy. The Twentieth Century Blues is a disease of the soul rather than the mind; a disorder of the spirit rather than the body. There is no chemical or biochemical abnormality associated with it. Inevitably, therefore, there is no *medical* cure for this condition.

Toxic stress cannot be treated as a medical problem and The Twentieth Century Blues cannot be cured with traditional therapies. Toxic stress is a force which affects the soul and since The Twentieth Century Blues is an affliction of the spirit rather than the body, the answer lies outside orthodox medical thinking.

To find out just how much stress is affecting your health and your life – and to find out whether or not you are suffering from The Twentieth Century Blues – answer the questions in the questionnaire on page 50.

When you have finished the questionnaire, keep a record of your Stress Vulnerability Score (SVS). You should repeat it every week and keep a note of your score either on the special Personal Stress Record Planner (on page 52) or, if you don't want to mark the book, on a piece of paper. After a few months your chart should show how successful your attempts to control your stress have been.

KNOW THE BOTTOM LINE

Fear of the unknown is a destructive, disabling and sometimes crippling force. Fear of what *may* happen is likely to stop you doing many of the things you might otherwise enjoy or benefit from.

You can conquer this fear by using your imagination to discover the worst that can happen. Strangely, the truth is that the worst that can happen is usually nowhere near as bad as you might fear.

CASE HISTORY

Kate suffered a lot with her nerves and most of her problems were a result of the job she had. She found the work unpleasant but, most of all, she disliked the man for whom she worked. She didn't leave the company because she had worked there for 15 years and was frightened of what would happen if she lost her job. She lived with her elderly mother and their three cats and they needed the money she earned. Kate assumed that if she lost her job, she and her mother would starve. She always assumed that she needed her boss more than he needed her. She lived in fear of him and never dared object when her boss wanted her to work late for no extra pay.

One day Kate sat down and carefully examined her greatest fear: what would happen if she lost her job.

The more she thought about it, the more she realized that the unknown was not as terrifying as she had imagined. She realized that she had numerous well-sought after skills. When she looked in the 'jobs vacant' section of the local newspaper she discovered that there were plenty of firms advertising for people like her.

Kate found the bottom line, and she realized that it wasn't as frightening as she had feared. She applied for another, better paid job that looked more interesting. She got it, and handed in her notice.

Her boss, suddenly realizing just how much he needed her, offered to increase her salary and holidays and add an annual bonus. But Kate wasn't interested. When she left, she realized that *he* needed her far more than *she* needed him.

If you have any terrible fear which haunts you, try to confront it. Try to work out what is the *worst* that can happen. Try to define the bottom line. It is hardly ever as bad as you think it's going to be.

HOW WORRYING MORE CAN HELP YOU WORRY LESS

Do you worry about everything? If so, then you may be able to help yourself by taking your worrying more seriously – and spending more time on it.

People who allocate fixed amounts of time for worrying suffer less torment – and fewer physical side effects of stress – than people who try to push their worries into the background.

Most people who worry a lot worry in bits. Ask yourself these questions:

1. Would you describe yourself as a 'worrier'?
2. Do you worry about unimportant things?
3. Do your worries come and go endlessly?
4. Do your worries ever stop you getting to sleep?
5. Do you rarely get the chance to think your worries through to a logical conclusion?

If you have answered 'yes' to any of these questions then you would almost certainly suffer far less if you allocated a firm 30 minutes a day for worrying.

TRY THIS SIMPLE WORRY DETOX PROGRAMME:

• **Keep a notebook and a pencil handy and write down every worry that comes into your mind. Unless a problem is really urgent, put it on one side to wait for your special 30 minute 'worry session'.**
• **When you know you can find 30 minutes for specialized worrying, turn off the telephone and go somewhere quiet where you won't be disturbed.**
• **Concentrate hard on each item on your list. Try to look at each problem from new angles. If other people are involved try to see things from their point of view.**
• **Where you can, write down solutionss.**
• **Now put your worries in order of importance.**
• **Now go through each worry on your list and ask yourself: 'What is the worst that can happen?'**

Most of the worries which can irritate and create tension can be thought through quite quickly when you spend time on them. By concentrating hard on your worries you will get a chance to put them into perspective. And you will be surprised at how many answers you find and how many problems simply disappear when thought through properly.

ARE YOU SUFFERING FROM STRESS BURN-OUT AND THE TWENTIETH CENTURY BLUES?

1. ARE YOU IRRITABLE, PICKY AND BAD TEMPERED?

0 for 'never'
1 for 'occasionally
2 for 'often'
3 for 'frequently'
4 for 'all the time'

2. DO YOU FEEL BORED BY YOUR LIFE?

0 for 'never'
1 for 'occasionally'
2 for 'often'
3 for 'frequently'
4 for 'all the time'

3. DO YOU BELIEVE THAT YOU ARE INDISPENSABLE?

0 for 'no'
3 for 'yes'

4. DO YOU WISH YOU COULD JUST RUN AWAY FROM EVERYTHING?

0 for 'never'
2 for 'occasionally'
4 for 'often'
6 for 'frequently'
8 for 'all the time'

5. DO YOU CONSTANTLY FEEL RUSHED – UNABLE TO FIND THE TIME TO DO ALL THE THINGS YOU FEEL YOU OUGHT TO DO, LET ALONE THE THINGS THAT YOU WOULD LIKE TO DO?

0 for 'no'
6 for 'yes'

6. DO YOU OFTEN FEEL THAT YOU OUGHT TO BE DOING MORE WITH YOUR LIFE?

0 for 'no'
6 for 'yes'

7. DO YOU FEEL DISSATISFIED WITH YOUR LIFE WITHOUT REALLY KNOWING WHY?

0 for 'no'
6 for 'yes'

8. HAVE YOU LOST INTEREST IN SEX?

0 for 'no'
1 for 'occasionally'
2 for 'often'
3 for 'frequently'
4 for 'all the time'

9. DO YOU FEEL – INEXPLICABLY – THAT YOU ARE UNDER THE WEATHER (AS THOUGH YOU ARE RECOVERING FROM THE 'FLU)?

0 for 'no'
2 for 'occasionally'
4 for 'often'
6 for 'frequently'
8 for 'all the time'

10. DO YOU SUFFER FROM ANY OF THE SYMPTOMS OR DISEASES LISTED ON PAGE 20?:
(score 1 point for each)

11. DO YOU WORRY UNREASONABLY ABOUT TRIVIAL, INSIGNIFICANT THINGS THAT IN YOUR HEART YOU KNOW DON'T REALLY MATTER?

0 for 'no'
2 for 'occasionally'
4 for 'often'
6 for 'frequently'
8 for 'all the time'

12. TO GET THROUGH THE DAY DO YOU NEED:
(SCORE 2 POINTS FOR EACH 'YES' ANSWER)

• alcohol
• tobacco
• coffee
• tranquillizers
• sleeping pills
• other prescribed drugs
• illegal drugs

13. DO YOU FIND IT DIFFICULT TO TAKE AN INTEREST IN YOUR WORK?

0 for 'no'
2 for 'occasionally'
4 for 'often'
6 for 'frequently'
8 for 'all the time'

14. DO YOU FIND IT DIFFICULT TO TAKE AN INTEREST IN HOBBIES THAT YOU USED TO ENJOY?

0 for 'no'
2 for 'occasionally'
4 for 'often'
6 for 'frequently'
8 for 'all the time'

15. DO YOU SUFFER MUCH FROM SYMPTOMS AND AILMENTS FOR WHICH THERE NEVER SEEMS TO BE ANY COMPLETELY SATISFACTORY TREATMENT?
0 for 'no'
6 for 'yes'

16. DO ANY SYMPTOMS AND ILLNESSES WHICH YOU GET SEEM TO LINGER APPARENTLY ENDLESSLY?
0 for 'no'
6 for 'yes'

17. DO YOU FEEL NERVOUS OR ANXIOUS EVEN THOUGH YOU KNOW THAT YOU DON'T REALLY HAVE ANYTHING TO BE NERVOUS OR ANXIOUS ABOUT?
0 for 'no'
2 for 'occasionally'
4 for 'often'
6 for 'frequently'
8 for 'all the time'

18. DO YOU EVER FEEL STRANGELY AND INEXPLICABLY ALONE?
0 for 'no'
6 for 'yes'

19. DO YOU EVER GO FOR WHOLE DAYS WITHOUT FEELING HAPPY OR GLAD TO BE ALIVE?
0 for 'no'
4 for 'yes'

20. DO YOU EVER FEEL A COMPLETE SENSE OF DESPAIR ABOUT THE FUTURE OF THE WORLD?
0 for 'no'
4 for 'yes'

21. WOULD YOU LIKE TO LIVE FOR EVER?
0 for 'yes'
6 for 'no'

22. DO YOU HAVE DIFFICULTY IN RELAXING?
0 for 'no'
6 for 'yes'

23. DO YOU HAVE DIFFICULTY IN GETTING STARTED IN THE MORNINGS?
0 for 'no'
4 for 'yes'

24. DO YOU GET TEARFUL (FOR NO VERY GOOD REASON)?
0 for 'no'
1 for 'occasionally'
2 for 'often'
3 for 'frequently'
4 for 'all the time'

25. DO YOU WORRY ABOUT YOUR HEALTH?
0 for 'no'
1 for 'occasionally'
2 for 'often'
3 for 'frequently'
4 for 'all the time'

26. DO YOU HAVE ANY DREAMS OR HOPES FOR THE FUTURE?
0 for 'yes'
4 for 'no'

27. DO YOU HAVE DIFFICULTY IN TELLING PEOPLE HOW YOU FEEL ABOUT THINGS?
0 for 'no'
4 for 'yes'

28. DO YOU GET EASILY UPSET WHEN THINGS BREAK DOWN?
0 for 'no'
4 for 'yes'

29. DO YOU EVER FEEL SO FULL OF FRUSTRATION AND ANGER THAT YOU WANT TO SCREAM AND SHOUT?
0 for 'no'
1 for 'occasionally'
2 for 'often'
3 for 'frequently'
4 for 'all the time'

SEE OVERLEAF TO SEE HOW YOU HAVE SCORED

IF YOU SCORED BETWEEN 0 AND 5 THEN YOU ARE SUFFERING VERY LITTLE FROM STRESS – THOUGH YOU SHOULD SEE YOUR DOCTOR ABOUT ANY SYMPTOMS OR ANXIETIES.

IF YOU SCORED BETWEEN 6 AND 99 THEN YOU ARE SUFFERING FROM EARLY BURN-OUT. TAKE IMMEDIATE STEPS TO LIMIT YOUR EXPOSURE TO STRESS AND TO IMPROVE YOUR ABILITY TO DEAL WITH STRESSFUL EVENTS. TALK TO YOUR DOCTOR AND READ THIS BOOK CAREFULLY.

IF YOU SCORED OVER 100 THEN YOU ARE SUFFERING FROM THE TWENTIETH CENTURY BLUES. TALK TO YOUR DOCTOR AS SOON AS YOU CAN AND READ THE REST OF THIS BOOK CAREFULLY. MAKE EVERY EFFORT TO INCREASE YOUR MENTAL STRENGTH AND TO REDUCE YOUR EXPOSURE TO UNNECESSARY STRESS.

PERSONAL STRESS RECORD PLANNER

DATE STRESS VULNERABILITY SCORE

9.4.96   98.

TIPS FOR DEALING WITH THE TWENTIETH CENTURY BLUES

If you are suffering from The Twentieth Century Blues please don't despair. There are things you can do to change the way you feel. Because The Twentieth Century Blues is basically a disease of the spirit you need to change some long-established attitudes and to acquire a new understanding of yourself and the world you live in.

• Refuse to allow yourself to be trapped by society's lunatic values. Many people do things – and buy things – because they are trying to impress people they don't even know. Don't let that happen to you. When you find yourself buying something you know you don't need, ask yourself who you are trying to impress. And then ask yourself whether or not you really care what they think about you.

• Share your feelings with the people around you. If you love someone, tell him – or her. If you are angry, then say so. We live in the communications age but too few people *communicate* with one another. Learn to listen and you will learn a lot.

• Learn as much as you can about yourself. Learn about your strengths and your weaknesses, your ambitions, needs, likes and dislikes. Ask yourself how others see you. The more you know about yourself, the stronger you will become.

• If you have any terrible fear which haunts you, try to confront; try to define the bottom line. Try to work out what is the worst that can happen. You will probably surprise yourself. The bottom line is hardly ever as bad as you think it's going to be.

• Give your life purpose. Once your life has purpose you will be inspired by ambition and hope. Your life needs some sort of purpose as much as it needs food, water and oxygen. You need to be stretched, you need to take chances and you need to know that your life is worthwhile.

MEASURE YOUR EXPOSURE TO STRESS

ANSWER THE FOLLOWING QUESTIONS TO FIND OUT JUST HOW MUCH STRESS THERE IS IN YOUR LIFE AT THE MOMENT. IF YOUR ANSWER IS 'YES' TO TWO QUESTIONS BECAUSE OF THE SAME PROBLEM YOU SHOULD STILL SCORE TWICE; YOU MAY HAVE BEEN IN TROUBLE WITH THE POLICE AND SEEN A LAWYER IN THE LAST THREE MONTHS FOR THE SAME OFFENCE.

1. HAVE YOU GOT ENGAGED OR MARRIED WITHIN THE LAST:
a) 6 months (4 points)
b) 12 months (3 points)
c) 18 months (2 points)
d) 24 months (1 point)

2. HAVE YOU BEEN INVOLVED IN THE BREAK UP OF A SERIOUS RELATIONSHIP WITHIN THE LAST:
a) 6 months (4 points)
b) 12 months (3 points)
c) 18 months (2 points)
d) 24 months (1 point)

3. HAS ANYONE CLOSE TO YOU DIED WITHIN THE LAST:
a) 6 months (4 points)
b) 12 months (3 points)
c) 18 months (2 points)
d) 24 months (1 point)

4. HAVE YOU MOVED HOUSE OR HAD MAJOR BUILDING WORK WITHIN THE LAST:
a) 6 months (4 points)
b) 12 months (3 points)
c) 18 months (2 points)
d) 24 months (1 point)

5. HAVE YOU BEEN SERIOUSLY ILL WITHIN THE LAST:
a) 6 months (4 points)
b) 12 months (3 points)
c) 18 months (2 points)
d) 24 months (1 point)

6. HAVE YOU NEEDED TO HAVE HOSPITAL TESTS WITHIN THE LAST:
a) 3 months (4 points)
b) 6 months (3 points)
c) 9 months (2 points)
d) 12 months (1 point)

7. HAVE YOU NEEDED TO SEE A LAWYER WITHIN THE LAST:
a) 3 months (4 points)
b) 6 months (3 points)
c) 9 months (2 points)
d) 12 months (1 point)

8. HAVE YOU BEEN IN TROUBLE WITH THE POLICE WITHIN THE LAST:
a) 6 months (4 points)
b) 12 months (3 points)
c) 18 months (2 points)
d) 24 months (1 point)

9. HAVE YOU LOST OR CHANGED YOUR JOB WITHIN THE LAST:
a) 6 months (4 points)
b) 12 months (3 points)
c) 18 months (2 points)
d) 24 months (1 point)

10. HAVE YOU INHERITED OR LOST A SIZEABLE SUM OF MONEY WITHIN THE LAST:
A) 3 MONTHS (4 POINTS)
B) 6 MONTHS (3 POINTS)
C) 9 MONTHS (2 POINTS)
D) 12 MONTHS (1 POINT)

IF YOU SCORED **10** OR MORE THEN YOU ARE CURRENTLY HIGHLY EXPOSED TO STRESS. TRY TO MANAGE YOUR LIFE SO THAT YOUR EXPOSURE TO STRESS IS REDUCED AND TRY ALSO TO BUILD UP YOUR RESISTANCE TO STRESS.

CHAPTER SIX

Why Drugs Are Not The Answer

The biggest drug addiction problem in the world today involves legally prescribed benzodiazepine tranquillizers and sleeping tablets, which are widely and regularly prescribed for long periods for men, women and children, suffering from stress and stress-related symptoms.

It seems hard to believe, but I first wrote about the dangers of tranquillizer addiction back in 1973. After hundreds of articles and TV programmes, my campaign to warn patients and doctors about the dangers of these drugs eventually forced the politicians to take action.

"The biggest drug addiction problem in the world today involves legally prescribed benzodiazepine tranquillizers and sleeping tablets"

In 1988 – after 15 years of campaigning – doctors were warned of the hazards of handing out drugs such as diazepam, lorazepam, nitrazepam and temazepam for long-term use.

But not all doctors read official warnings. And not all governments have followed Britain's example. And so tens of thousands of doctors are still handing out tranquillizers and sleeping tablets to millions of patients who have too much stress in their lives.

The simple truth is that the benzodiazepine tranquillizers can cause all sorts of problems if they are taken for more than two weeks or so. Long-term use can cause all sorts of very real problems. Patients who have been taking the drugs for more than a week or two, need to cut down slowly if they are to avoid withdrawal symptoms.

There are dozens of different drugs in this group. But some of the best known and most frequently prescribed benzodiazepine tranquillizers and sleeping tablets include: temazepam, nitrazepam, diazepam, lorazepam, flurazepam, chlordiazepoxide, triazolam, potassium clorazepate, oxazepam, lormetazepam. You should check with your doctor if you are in doubt about whether you are taking a benzodiazepine.

HERE ARE *SOME* OF THE WARNINGS GIVEN BY THE MANUFACTURERS OF A WELL-KNOWN BENZODIAZEPINE:

- *SYMPTOMS SUCH AS ANXIETY, DEPRESSION, HEADACHE, INSOMNIA, TENSION AND SWEATING HAVE BEEN REPORTED FOLLOWING ABRUPT DISCONTINUATION OF BENZODIAZEPINES. OTHER REPORTED SYMPTOMS INCLUDE TINNITUS, INVOLUNTARY MOVEMENTS, CONFUSION, CONVULSIONS, MUSCLE CRAMPS, ABDOMINAL CRAMPS AND VOMITING.*

- **PATIENTS TAKING THE DRUG MAY BECOME DIZZY OR DROWSY AND SHOULD BE WARNED AGAINST DRIVING OR OPERATING MACHINERY.**

- *ELDERLY PATIENTS MAY NEED TO BE GIVEN SMALLER DOSES. THEY MAY BE MORE SENSITIVE TO THE DRUG.*

- **THE USE OF BENZODIAZEPINES MAY RELEASE SUICIDAL IMPULSES IN DEPRESSED PATIENTS.**

- *BEHAVIOURAL EFFECTS OF THE DRUG INCLUDE EXCITEMENT, AGGRESSIVE OUTBURSTS AND CONFUSION. LOSS OF MEMORY MAY OCCUR.*

- **OTHER REPORTED SIDE EFFECTS INCLUDE: HANGOVER, HEADACHE ON WAKING, DIZZINESS, BLURRED VISION, NAUSEA, DEPRESSION, CHANGES IN APPETITE, SLEEP DISTURBANCE, BLOOD PROBLEMS, VISUAL DISTURBANCES, LOW BLOOD PRESSURE, INTESTINAL DISTURBANCES AND SKIN RASHES.**

For many years now, I have repeatedly warned that drugs in the benzodiazepine group are being wildly overprescribed and can cause tremendous problems. I have on many occasions also warned that drug abuse experts have told me that getting patients off these drugs is frequently more difficult than getting patients off other addictive drugs such as heroin. Sadly, it seems that, although some doctors now accept that benzodiazepines can cause problems, there are still doctors in practice who do not understand the problems the benzodiazepines can produce. If you see a doctor who tells you that the benzodiazepines never cause problems, don't cause addiction and can be stopped suddenly without danger my advice is: *change your doctor fast.*

Here, for the record, are some facts about tranquillizers which some doctors still don't seem to know. Look at the dates carefully.

FACT ONE In 1961, just a short time after chlordiazepoxide (the first widely prescribed benzodiazepine) had been introduced into clinical practice, a report was written by three physicians from a hospital in California. Entitled 'Withdrawal Reactions from Chlordiazepoxide' the paper described very dramatically how patients who had been taking the drug suffered from withdrawal symptoms when the drug was stopped. The authors described how 11 patients who had been taking fairly high doses of chlordiazepoxide for up to six months were quite suddenly taken off the drug and given sugar tablets instead. Ten of the 11 patients experienced new symptoms or signs after the withdrawal of the chlordiazepoxide. Six patients became depressed, five were agitated and unable to sleep, two had major fits.

FACT TWO Testifying to a U.S. Senate Health subcommittee in Washington in 1979, a psychiatrist claimed that patients could get hooked on diazepam in as little as six weeks. The same committee heard testimony that it is harder to kick the tranquillizer habit than it is to get off heroin.

FACT THREE In 1975 three doctors from the Drug Dependence Treatment Center at the Philadelphia VA Hospital and University of Pennsylvania, Philadelphia, published a paper in the *International Journal of Addictions* entitled 'Misuse and Abuse of Diazepam: An Increasingly Common Medical Problem'. The three authors of the paper referred to papers published as far back as 1970 which had documented instances of physical addiction to chlordiazepoxide and diazepam and reported that since the end of 1972 they had noticed an increasing amount of diazepam misuse and abuse. Their paper concluded: 'All physicians should know that diazepam abuse and misuse is occurring and careful attention should be given to prescribing, transporting and storing this drug.'

FACT FOUR In 1972 the *American Journal of Psychiatry* published a paper in which two doctors described how patients on diazepam had exhibited a cluster of symptoms which included tremulousness, apprehension, insomnia and depression. The patients had all been previously emotionally stable and the symptoms, which started suddenly, were quite severe. When these patients were taken off their diazepam their symptoms disappeared.

FACT FIVE In 1968 the *Journal of the American Medical Association* described a series of eight patients who had been given diazepam. The patients became so depressed that seven of them had suicidal thoughts and impulses and two of them made serious attempts to commit suicide.

FACT SIX Several reports published in the 1960s and 1970s showed that the benzodiazepines seemed to increase hostility, aggressiveness and irritability. The benzodiazepines have also been associated with baby battering.

FACT SEVEN In a paper published in 1979, researchers found a 'highly significant association between the use of minor tranquillizers and the risk of a serious road accident'. The conclusion was that a patient's risk of being involved in a serious accident was increased five-fold if he or she was taking a benzodiazepine. Many doctors now believe that thousands of acidents have been caused by drivers who have been taking benzodiazepines.

FACT EIGHT A researcher who claimed that benzodiazepines were related to the development of cancer complained that he was 'forced out of his research position'.

FACT NINE Back in 1982 the Committee on Safety of Medicines advised doctors that the benzodiazepines should be prescribed for short periods only, and that withdrawal symptoms could be avoided by withdrawing medication slowly.

FACT TEN When a 75-year-old lady was admitted to hospital in Newcastle-upon-Tyne in the early 1970s, she was unable to walk or speak clearly, and was confused and incontinent. She had been taking a benzodiazepine sleeping tablet for a year. When her pills were stopped she made a physical recovery in just three days.

The sad truth is that for years any doctor who has studied the medical journals has known that the benzodiazepines cause problems, but some doctors are still prescribing these damned pills by the lorry load.

'The world's biggest addiction problem is not teenagers taking hash but middle-agers taking sedatives. The tranquillizer is replacing tabacco. It will, perhaps, give us an even bigger problem. It may prove even more dangerous. Already Valium is said to be taken by 14 per cent of the population of Britain.'

'The habit usually starts insidiously. The patient may have a good excuse for taking a few tablets. A close friend or relative has died or there is a rush on at work - and the doctor finds it difficult to refuse the request for alittle help.'

Quote taken from *The Medicine Men* by Dr. Vernon Coleman, 1975

THE VICTIMS

During my campaign to get these drugs controlled more effectively – and to persuade doctors to prescribe them more carefully – I have received tens of thousands of letters from tranquillizer addicts all over the world. In one month alone, I counted over 6,000 letters.

The mail I have received has brought tears to my eyes and yet made me angry and indignant; made me feel frustrated and incapable, and yet given me the determination to continue to fight against these drugs.

Below are just a few extracts from some of the letters I have received. In my experience, patients constantly worry that they are the only ones ever to have suffered; they feel that they must be in some way responsible for their own problems. Knowing that countless others have suffered – and are still suffering – the same symptoms does seem to help.

'When I told my doctor that I thought I was addicted he told me not to be so silly and, if it bothered me that much to simply stop taking them.'

'I am unable to stop. My husband doesn't understand and I find myself sneaking the tablets into my handbag because if he catches me taking them he calls me a drug addict.'

'I was suffering from stress when I went to my doctor and now I'm hooked. I used to be a friendly, outgoing sort of person. But my life has been destroyed.'

'On numerous occasions I have tried to get off them. I can only describe the terrible pains and the awful feelings as being like hell on earth.'

'My problem started five years ago with post natal depression. At first the pills were great. But the trouble started when I tried to get off them and found I couldn't live without them. I swear to God I have never in all my life felt so scared. I attempted suicide but couldn't go through with it.'

WHY DID THE BENZODIAZEPINES BECOME SO POPULAR?

During the 1950s and 1960s, family doctors found that they were expected to deal with mental and psychological problems, as well as physical problems. They were, for the first time, consulted by patients who wanted comfort, encouragement and help with social and personal problems. As the link between stress and disease became better known, so more patients went to their doctors wanting help with dealing with stress.

But there was a problem. Doctors had never been trained to cope with psychological or stress-induced problems. Most had been taught more about tropical diseases than they had about anxiety or depression.

So, when the benzodiazepines were introduced and described as safe and effective drugs for the treatment of anxiety and a wide range of stress-related disorders,

ARE YOU A TRANQUILLIZER ADDICT?

To find out whether or not you are addicted to a tranquillizer or sleeping tablet answer 'yes' or 'no' to the following questions. If you answer 'yes' to any of these questions, then you are probably hooked and you should take special care before stopping your pills.

1. Do you obtain your pills on repeat prescription without seeing your doctor?

2. Do you worry if your supply of pills gets low?

3. If you go out of the house do you have to take some of your pills with you?

4. If you miss a pill do you suffer any unusual or unpleasant symptoms?

5. Have any of your original symptoms – the reason why you started taking the pills – got worse?

6. Have you been taking a tranquillizer or sleeping tablet for three months or more?

7. Have you needed to increase your dose of the drug since you first started?

8. Has your doctor had to change your brand?

9. Do you still have any of the symptoms for which the pills were originally prescribed?

10. Do you persistently suffer from drowsiness, tiredness, lethargy or unsteadiness?

Tips for coming off tranquillizers

If you are hooked on a benzodiazepine tranquillizer or sleeping tablet, you will need to wean yourself off your drug with care. Here are some vital tips.

1. Before doing anything, visit your doctor and ask for his or her help. If he is unhelpful, if he tells you to cope by yourself or if he insists that you don't need to worry and that withdrawal is easy, then I suggest that you find yourself a new doctor.

2. You may experience unpleasant symptoms (see list on page 61). Be prepared.

3. Remember that you can minimize your symptoms by reducing your dose slowly. The rate at which you reduce your pills, will depend upon the size of the dosage you have been taking and the length of time for which you have been on the pills.

4. Remember that the benzodiazepines cure nothing. But they do cover symptoms up. If you originally took your tablets for anxiety then the chances are that your original symptoms will return when you stop taking the tablets.

5. Warn your family and friends that you are likely to be going through a difficult time.

6. Do not try to give up these pills if you are going through a tricky patch at home or at work.

7. Do not be tempted to try carving your tablets into tiny pieces. Break them into half by all means. But carving pills into fractions tends to make the whole procedure more difficult. It also makes everything more dramatic. Ask your doctor to prescribe the lowest dose of pills available so that you have the maximum amount of flexibility.

8. Do not despair if you reach a plateau and have difficulty in reducing your pills any more. Do not even despair if you have to increase your pills temporarily. You must stop these drugs at a rate that you find comfortable.

9. If you are taking a drug like lorazepam – which many experts believe is particularly difficult to come off – then your doctor may recommend that you substitute diazepam for part of the lorazepam and then cut down both drugs gradually. This *must* be done under medical supervision.

10. If you know someone else who wants to kick the habit then plan to do it together. Ring one another up, keep in touch, share your problems and keep your determination alive.

If you want to try a really gradual cutting down technique your doctor may suggest that you try the 'staging' technique. If, for example, you were taking three tablets a day to start with your routine would look something like this:

DAY/S	TABLET/S
1	THREE
2	TWO
3 - 7	THREE
8	TWO
9 - 12	THREE
13	TWO
14 - 16	THREE
17	TWO
18 & 19	THREE
20	TWO
21	THREE
22 - 26	TWO
27	ONE
28 - 31	TWO
32	ONE
33 - 35	TWO
36	ONE
37 - 38	TWO
39	ONE
40	TWO
41 - 45	ONE
46	NONE
47 - 50	ONE
51	NONE
52 - 54	ONE
55	NONE
56 - 57	ONE
58	NONE
59	ONE
60	NONE

Continue with a reduction to half a tablet. The advantage of this system is that it gives your body plenty of time to get used to each new step down. Obviously, the same technique can be adapted to suit any patient on any starting dose.

How long does withdrawal last?

This is the question tranquillizer addicts ask most often, and it is the one that causes most controversy.

Some experts claim that withdrawal should take no more than a few weeks. One expert I know says that it can last for 10 per cent of the time for which pills were taken. Some former addicts claim that it has taken them years to get off their pills.

The truth is that there is no fixed time for withdrawal. Some people can do it in days. Some take months. One reason for some of the confusion is that doctors and patients are sometimes talking about two quite separate things when they talk about withdrawal.

When drug addiction experts talk about the length of time it takes to come off tranquillizers they are talking about the period of time over which physical withdrawal needs to be spread. To keep physical withdrawal – the symptoms produced by the body being deprived of the drug – to an absolute minimum, the drug needs to be cut down slowly.

'But,' say these experts, 'it is important not to spread the physical withdrawal over too long a period.' If the pills are cut down too slowly, then the patient will be taking the drug for longer than is necessary. 'The quicker you stop the pills,' the argument goes, 'the quicker you will recover. Spread the withdrawal over too long and your recovery will be slow.'

Patients sometimes respond to this by pointing out that although they cut down their pills in a matter of weeks they are still getting side effects months later. This, however, does not necessarily mean that these side effects are withdrawal effects. The whole picture is confused by several other factors.

First, it is important to remember that the benzodiazepines do not cure anything. If you were put on a tranquillizer ten years ago because you were feeling anxious and unhappy then the pills will have numbed your mind for ten years – but they will not have stopped your initial problem. When you stop taking the pills, your old anxiety will still be there. While you were taking the pills you may not have noticed the anxiety symptoms.

If you were given your pills 15 years ago to cover up the unhappiness of a bereavement, then you will once more have to endure the unhappiness of that bereavement. The benzodiazepines will have put your emotions into a sort of pharmacological 'deep-freeze'.

Second, although the benzodiazepines do not cure anything, they do numb the mind. They seal you off from the world around you and prevent you from experiencing the normal highs and lows of everyday life. Taking these drugs is like having your brain wrapped in a thick layer of cotton wool. While taking the drug you are immune to many of the pressures of everyday living; the world will be uniformly grey; you will be permanently anaethetized.

Once you stop taking your pills, your mind will suddenly be exposed to a whole range of stimuli. The anaesthetic will 'wear off' and you will 'wake up'. It can certainly be a frightening experience. The world will suddenly appear a good deal brighter. Noises will seem louder and joys and sorrows will seem more acute. So, in addition to having to cope with old, half-forgotten emotions and sensations, you will find that your nerve endings are raw and easily stimulated.

Since all these symptoms occur immediately after stopping or cutting down the pills, you will probably assume that the symptoms have developed because you have stopped your drug too quickly. I don't think that this is necessarily the case. The symptoms are an inevitable part of coming off tranquillizers, but they will be there, however slowly you reduce the dose. Extending the withdrawal period doesn't always affect the end result at all – it may merely prolong the agony.

Finally, it is essential that anyone planning to give up tranquillizers should spend a lot of time and effort learning how to relax and how to deal with stress.

> ### WARNING
> USING TRANQUILLIZERS OR SLEEPING TABLETS TO COMBAT THE EFFECTS OF STRESS IS LIKE WRAPPING A BLANKET ROUND A FIRE ALARM BECAUSE YOU DON'T LIKE THE NOISE.
> ### WARNING
> DO NOT STOP TAKING TRANQUILLIZERS OR SLEEPING TABLETS, OR TRY CUTTING DOWN, WITHOUT GETTING PROFESSIONAL HELP FROM YOUR DOCTOR.

WHAT WITHDRAWAL SYMPTOMS SHOULD YOU EXPECT?

SOME PEOPLE ARE LUCKY. THEY CAN STOP TAKING THESE DRUGS WITH RELATIVELY FEW – OR EVEN NO – SIDE EFFECTS. OTHERS ARE LESS FORTUNATE. HERE IS A FAIRLY COMPREHENSIVE LIST OF THE SIDE EFFECTS THAT PATIENTS HAVE COMPLAINED OF WHILE COMING OFF BENZODIAZEPINE TRANQUILLIZERS AND SLEEPING TABLETS.

SLEEPLESSNESS

LOSS OF APPETITE

THIRST

WEIGHT LOSS

VOMITING

NAUSEA

SORE TONGUE

DIFFICULTY IN SWALLOWING

METALLIC TASTE IN THE MOUTH

STOMACH CRAMPS

DIARRHOEA

CONSTIPATION

DIFFICULTY IN BREATHING

IRREGULAR BREATHING

TIGHT CHEST

RAPID BREATHING

DRY COUGH

IRREGULAR PULSE

ALTERED BLOOD PRESSURE

PALPITATIONS

SWOLLEN HANDS, FACE OR FEET

TREMORS AND SHAKES

HAIR LOSS

CRACKED LIPS

CORNERS OF MOUTH CRACKED

SEXUAL DESIRE CHANGED (REDUCED OR INCREASED)

CHANGES IN MENSTRUATION

INCREASED VAGINAL SECRETION

SWOLLEN VULVA

FITS

INCONTINENCE

DIFFICULTY IN PASSING URINE

POOR CONCENTRATION

LACK OF DRIVE

LACK OF INITIATIVE

ANXIETY

PANIC

GUILT

SADNESS, DESPAIR AND DEPRESSION

WANTING TO COMMIT SUICIDE

LACK OF CONFIDENCE

IRRITABILITY

A FEAR OF GOING INSANE

AGGRESSION AND RAGE

RESTLESSNESS

VOLATILE EMOTIONS

LACK OF A SENSE OF HUMOUR

ATTENTION SEEKING

BEING DEMANDING AND GIVING OTHER PEOPLE A HARD TIME

BEING QUARRELSOME

HAVING DESTRUCTIVE THOUGHTS

TENSION IN THE HEAD, NECK AND SHOULDERS

BACKACHE

SLURRED SPEECH

STUTTERING

WORD CONFUSION

PINS AND NEEDLES

HOT AND COLD SHIVERS

DIFFICULTY IN SWALLOWING

SHIVERING

FATIGUE AND EXHAUSTION

FEELING OF HAVING A TIGHT BAND AROUND THE HEAD

NUMB HANDS AND FEET

UNSTEADINESS

HALLUCINATIONS

PARANOIA

NIGHTMARES

RELIVING THE PAST

PAINS AROUND THE MOUTH

HYPERSENSITIVITY TO TOUCH, SMELL, LIGHT OR NOISE

NOISES IN THE EARS (TINNITUS)

A FEELING OF UNREALITY

DEPERSONALIZATION (A FEELING OF BEING UNREAL IN ONE'S OWN BODY)

VISUAL DISTURBANCES – OBJECTS SEEMING SMALLER OR LARGER

BLURRED VISION AND OTHER VISUAL PROBLEMS

NOTE

THIS CHAPTER REFERS TO TRANQUILLIZERS AND SLEEPING TABLETS WHICH ARE WIDELY PRESCRIBED FOR ANXIETY AND STRESS RELATED DISORDERS. IT DOES NOT REFER TO ANTIDEPRESSANTS WHICH ARE QUITE DIFFERENT DRUGS. ALL PRESCRIPTION DRUGS SHOULD BE TAKEN ACCORDING TO A DOCTOR'S ADVICE AND YOU SHOULD NEVER STOP TAKING ANY DRUG THAT HAS BEEN PRESCRIBED FOR YOU WITHOUT FIRST TALKING TO YOUR DOCTOR.

CHAPTER SEVEN

How To Build Up Your Self-Confidence

Advice about how to cope with stress and about how to deal with anxiety is frequently rather vague and simplistic. Too often, doctors and others will merely tell a patient suffering from a stress-related disorder that she or he must spend some time relaxing. That isn't a lot of help, of course. Most people assume that they are relaxing when they are slumped in front of the television set – but they aren't. Just sitting down and trying (usually in vain) to ignore the day's problems won't help at all.

If you are going to deal effectively with stress and cope efficiently with anxiety, you have to do a more than that. You have to learn how to use the power of your own mind constructively.

"Your imagination can make you ill – but it can make you well again too"

Don't forget that it is your mind's ability to exaggerate problems and to see the worst possible outcome that helped to create your feelings of anxiety. It is your mind which makes you susceptible to stress and pressure and, if you know how to use it properly, your mind can also defend you against stress and immunize you against the unpleasant consequences of anxiety. Your imagination can make you ill – but it can make you well again too; it can make you weak but it can also make you strong.

All this may sound daunting and rather impossible. It isn't. It really is very simple.

To start with, one of the best ways to help yourself reduce your exposure to unnecessary and harmful stresses is to build up your own self-confidence. The more you can build up your confidence, the less susceptible you will be to guilt, destructive feelings of inadequacy and excessive self-criticism. You will also be stronger when you are confronted by people who want you to do things that you don't really want to do. All these things will help you deal far more effectively with stress, and will help to protect you from the harmful effects of stress.

Try sitting down with a piece of paper and a pencil and writing down all the good things you can think of to say about yourself. Imagine that you are preparing an advertising campaign for yourself. Throw modesty out of the window and try to promote all your virtues and good points. Imagine that you are trying to sell yourself to the world – though in reality, of course, all you are trying to do is to sell yourself to yourself.

Try to think of all the good words which describe you; honest, generous, thoughtful, hard-working, punctual, careful, considerate, moral, kind, ambitious, creative. Write down every good word that you think you can honestly apply to yourself. And don't be falsely modest – no one except you need ever see this list.

Make a list of all your assets too. I don't mean a crude list of the money you have and the things you own – though by all means do that if it will help you feel better – but a list of all the intangibles in your life: your partner, your children, your integrity, your friends, your interests, your knowledge, your accomplishments and your memories – particularly your memories. Those are the real valuables in your life.

If you lack self-confidence you will probably often worry about disastrous things happening to you; you may become almost irretrievably pessimistic. You can

Charles Bronson, a poor immigrant, had few advantages but became a Hollywood star

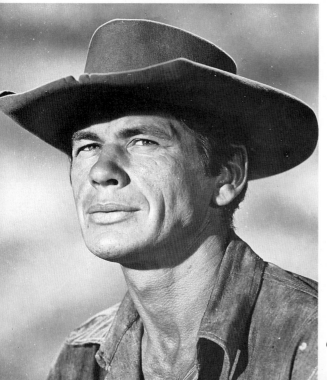

defuse this particular fear by always asking yourself: 'What is the worst thing that can happen in this situation?' You will frequently be surprised to find that the 'worst' really isn't all that bad. And once you know the worst you can make plans accordingly.

SEVEN WAYS TO BUILD UP YOUR SELF-CONFIDENCE

In order to build up your self-confidence you must replace negative, damaging feelings of failure, incompetence and unworthiness with positive feelings of success. Here are some practical ways in which you can boost your self-confidence:

1. **Write an advertisement extolling your virtues and listing all your good points. You can't think of any? Then look down this list and pick out the words which you honestly feel apply to you:**

• HONEST	• KIND
• TRUTHFUL	• CAREFUL
• ROMANTIC	• CREATIVE
• HONOURABLE	• AMBITIOUS
• PUNCTILIOUS	• HARD-WORKING
• SCRUPULOUS	• BRAVE
• ATTENTIVE	• WITTY
• FAITHFUL	• WISE
• DECENT	• INTELLIGENT
• MORAL	• POLITE
• CONSCIENTIOUS	• PUNCTUAL
• RESPECTABLE	• THOUGHTFUL
• LAW-ABIDING	• FASTIDIOUS
• CHIVALROUS	• AGREEABLE
• UNSELFISH	• WELCOMING
• IMPECCABLE	• SKILFUL
• OBEDIENT	
• BENEVOLENT	

2. **What is your worst fault? What is it that people accuse you of most frequently? (If you really don't know your worst fault, try to decide what you dislike most in other people –** *that* **is probably your worst fault!)**

Now try to turn your fault around and look at it from the other side. No personality is two-dimensional and on the reverse of every bad quality there is usually at least one good quality.

- If you are **obsessive** you are also likely to be observant, watchful and meticulous.
- If you are **impatient** you are also likely to be creative, energetic and full of energy.
- If you are **pessimistic** you are also likely to be cautious, sensible and reliable.
- If you are **irresponsible** you are also likely to be fun, and exciting to be with.
- If you are **impractical** you are also likely to be artistic, sensitive and imaginative.
- If you are **vain** you are also likely to be fastidious and conscientious.
- If you are **intolerant** you are also likely to be honourable, truthful and law-abiding.
- If you are **unromantic** you are also likely to be practical, sensible and down to earth.
- If you are **prudish** you are also likely to be faithful and virtuous.
- If you are **ruthless** you are also likely to be ambitious, and hard-working.
- If you are **shy** you are also likely to be sensitive, thoughtful and imaginative.
- If you are **sensitive** you are also likely to be polite, thoughtful, generous and unselfish.

3. If you are always worrying about your mistakes and if you seem to be forever apologizing, just remember that everyone makes mistakes occasionally. No one can possibly be right all the time. There is nothing wrong in saying 'I was wrong. I am sorry'. If you accept challenges, take risks and live your life to the full then sometimes you will fail. Occasionally, your judgements will be faulty. You, and those who have supported you, will

There is nothing wrong in saying 'I'm sorry!'

lose face. But, although making a mistake is a weakness, admitting that you have made a mistake is a sign of strength and courage. Remember that apologizing for your mistakes is a sign of maturity and learning from your mistakes is a sign of true wisdom. People who never make mistakes never take chances and people who never take chances have a life full of missed opportunities.

4. Don't be afraid to say 'I don't know'. However guilty you may feel at not knowing something, remember that admitting that you don't know is a sign of strength. No one can possibly know everything. The powerful, the wise and the great are always prepared to admit that there are boundaries to their knowledge. Only the weak, the uncertain and the stupid are silly and conceited enough to pretend that they know everything.

5. Learn to be more selfish. People who have a low self-esteem and who suffer a lot from guilt tend to be selfless – and tend to spend much of their lives worrying about and thinking about other people. If you are a guilt sufferer you probably need to spend more time thinking about what *you* want.

6. If you ever feel that your life is a failure and you wish that you had more to be proud of, make a list of all the things in your life that are really important to you: partner, friends, health, children, integrity, interests, knowledge and memories. You will probably be surprised to find how many things there are of which you can be proud!

7. When you are worried about the future, ask yourself what is the worst that can happen. You will probably be surprised to find that the 'worst' may not be as bad as you thought it was going to be. The 'bottom line' often isn't as daunting as you think it will be.

CHAPTER EIGHT

How To Relax Your Body

When you are anxious, nervous or under stress in any way, your mind deliberately tenses up the muscles around your body. There is a long-established, sensible reason for this. By tensing up muscles, your mind is preparing your body for action; it assumes that the best way to deal with the threat you are facing will be physical action. Your mind is getting your body ready to fight or to run away.

"Learning how to avoid unnecessary stresses, how to build up your resistance to stress and how to improve your ability to cope with stress will all help you combat muscle tension"

But most modern stresses cannot be dealt with by a physical response. You cannot fight a traffic jam and running away from an electricity bill won't do you any good. Modern stresses persist for long periods – and so muscles remain tense for long periods, too.

Tensed muscles commonly produce headaches, backache and stiff necks. As many as eight out of ten cases of backache are caused by stress, and a staggering 98 per cent of headaches are produced in the same way.

Learning how to avoid unnecessary stresses, how to build up your resistance to stress and how to improve your ability to cope with stress will all help you combat muscle tension.

But there is another, more direct way, to tackle muscle tension and the associated problems it produces – deliberately relaxing your tensed muscles.

Many people refuse to try to learn how to relax, wrongly believing that in order to relax your body you must be physically fit, unusually supple and agile. These fears are unjustified. *You* can learn how to relax your body quickly and easily if you follow the simple instructions on the pages which follow.

RELAXING YOUR BODY

THIS SIMPLE-TO-LEARN TECHNIQUE SHOULD HELP TO RELIEVE ANY TENSION IN YOUR MUSCLES. MAKE SURE THAT YOU WILL NOT BE DISTURBED FOR ABOUT 20 MINUTES. WEARING LOOSE, COMFORTABLE CLOTHES BUT NO SHOES LIE DOWN ON YOUR BACK IN A QUIET AND COMFORTABLE PLACE.

1. WHEN YOU ARE UNDER STRESS YOU BREATHE MORE QUICKLY THAN USUAL, SO BEGIN BY TAKING BIG, DEEP, SLOW BREATHS. THIS WILL SOOTHE YOUR MIND – AND YOUR BODY.

2. START BY TIGHTLY CLENCHING YOUR RIGHT HAND. SQUEEZE YOUR FINGERS INTO THE PALM OF YOUR HAND TO MAKE A FIST AND TRY TO GET THE MUSCLES AS TIGHT AS YOU CAN. IF YOU DO THIS PROPERLY YOU SHOULD SEE YOUR KNUCKLES GO WHITE. NOW RELAX YOUR HAND AND LET YOUR FINGERS GRADUALLY UNFOLD. AS YOU DO THIS THE MUSCLES OF YOUR HAND WILL GO FROM FEELING TENSE TO RELAXED.

3. NOW FOLLOW THIS PROCEDURE WITH THE OTHER MUSCLE GROUPS OF YOUR BODY. CONCENTRATE ON YOUR MUSCLES ONE BY ONE AS YOU TENSE AND RELAX EACH ONE.

4. BEND YOUR RIGHT ARM AND TRY TO MAKE YOUR RIGHT BICEPS MUSCLE AS BIG AND TIGHT AS YOU CAN. THEN RELAX IT AND LET THE MUSCLES EASE. WHEN YOUR ARM IS THOROUGHLY RELAXED, LET IT LIE COMFORTABLY ON THE FLOOR BY YOUR SIDE.

5. MAKE SURE YOU ARE STILL BREATHING DEEPLY AND REGULARLY. NOW REPEAT STAGES 2 AND 4 WITH YOUR LEFT HAND AND ARM.

6. CURL UP THE TOES IN YOUR RIGHT FOOT AND TRY TO MAKE THE MUSCLES AS TIGHT AS YOU CAN. NOW CURL YOUR TOES DOWNWARDS AS FAR AS YOU CAN. WHEN YOUR FOOT FEELS AS TENSE AS YOU CAN MAKE IT LET IT GO LOOSE AND RELAXED.

7. NOW MOVE ON TO YOUR RIGHT CALF AND TENSE THE MUSCLES AS TIGHTLY AS YOU CAN. IF YOU DO THIS PROPERLY YOUR CALF MUSCLES WILL BECOME QUITE FIRM AND HARD AS YOU TENSE THEM. BEND YOUR FOOT UP TOWARDS THE CEILING TO HELP TIGHTEN THE MUSCLES. THEN LET THE MUSCLES RELAX.

8. MAKE THE WHOLE OF YOUR RIGHT LEG AS STRAIGHT AS YOU CAN, POINTING YOUR TOES AWAY FROM YOU. YOU WILL FEEL THE MUSCLES ON THE FRONT OF YOUR RIGHT THIGH TIGHTEN UP. IF YOU TOUCH THEM THE MUSCLES SHOULD FEEL FIRM RIGHT UP TO THE TOP OF YOUR LEG. NOW RELAX THOSE MUSCLES AND LET YOUR LEG REST COMFORTABLY ON THE FLOOR.

9. NOW REPEAT STAGES 6, 7 AND 8 WITH YOUR LEFT FOOT, CALF AND WHOLE LEG. EACH TIME TENSE THE MUSCLES AS TIGHTLY AS YOU CAN FOR A FEW SECONDS BEFORE RELAXING.

10. TIGHTEN UP YOUR ABDOMINAL MUSCLES. MAKE A REAL EFFORT TO PULL YOUR TUMMY IN AS FAR AS YOU CAN. THEN REVERSE THE PROCESS, RELAX THE MUSCLES IN YOUR ABDOMEN AND LET YOUR TUMMY EXPAND AS MUCH AS IT WILL.

11. TIGHTEN UP YOUR BUTTOCK MUSCLES AND PUSH YOUR BOTTOM UP OFF THE FLOOR. IF YOU ARE DOING THIS EXERCISE PROPERLY YOU SHOULD BE ABLE TO LIFT YOUR BODY UPWARDS BY AN INCH OR SO. AFTER A FEW SECONDS LOWER YOURSELF BACK DOWN AND LET YOUR MUSCLES RELAX AGAIN.

12. Take a big, deep breath in and hold it for as long as possible. This will tighten up the muscles of your chest. Then, slowly, breathe out.

13. Now push your shoulders backwards into the floor as far as they will go, then bring them forwards and inwards. Finally, shrug them as high as you can. Try to keep your head as still as you can and try to touch your ears with your shoulders. It will probably be impossible but try anyway. Then let your shoulders relax and ease.

14. Try to make yourself as tall as you can by tightening up the muscles of your back and arching it slightly. Try to imagine you are being pulled in opposite directions at your feet and head. Then let the muscles relax.

15. The muscles of your neck are next. Lift your head up and forwards so that the muscles at the back of your neck are under tension. Turn your head first to the right and then to the left. Then push your head backwards with as much force as you can. Finally let the muscles of your neck relax by moving your head around in gentle circles.

16. Now concentrate on your face. Start by moving your eyebrows upwards and then pull them down as far as they will go into a deep frown. Do this several times, making sure that you can feel the muscles tightening both when you move your eyebrows up and when you pull them down. Then let them relax.

17. Pretend that you are trying to shut out the world and screw up your eyes as tightly as you can. Keep them shut tightly for a few seconds then, still keeping your eyelids closed, let the muscles around your eyes relax.

18. Wrinkle your nose. Grit your teeth. Move your lower jaw around, open your mouth as wide as you can then screw your lips up. Use all the muscles in and around your mouth. Finally poke your tongue out as far as it will go! Now relax.

Make your own relaxation tape

To make your own personal relaxation tape, slowly read out the 'Relaxing Your Body' script into a tape recorder. Then lie down, play back the tape and listen to it carefully. You'll find it much easier to listen to the instructions on a tape than to try and read them out of a book while you are relaxing. Do remember to read out the instructions fairly slowly, and to pause between each set of instructions. You may need one or two attempts to get it right.

Warning
When you have recorded your tape do **NOT** listen to it while driving or operating machinery since it may make you drowsy.

Too busy to relax?

Busy people often say that they are too busy to relax. They say that relaxing is a waste of time. They're wrong! Learning to relax is as essential for your mind as food is for your body.

CHAPTER NINE

Use Your Imagination To Conquer Anxiety

A patient of mine called E came to see me once complaining of an unpleasant skin rash that covered her arms, her neck and part of her chest. She undressed, lay down on the examination couch and showed me the rash.

'I don't know what's wrong with me,' she said, as I examined her. 'I've been getting terrible indigestion too. And normally I've got a cast iron digestive system.'

She sounded tired and looked as if she hadn't been sleeping very well. She had huge bags under her eyes and her hair looked dull and lifeless.

"It was worry that had made her irritable... and it was the worry which was causing the skin rash"

'Have you noticed anything else?' I asked her, when I had finished examining her. 'Apart from the skin rash and the indigestion?' My physical examination of her hadn't been of much use. I hadn't been able to find anything abnormal.

My patient didn't speak for a moment or two. 'I've been edgy for several weeks now,' she confessed at last. 'I've been taking it out on my husband and the children.' Suddenly, and quite unexpectedly, she started to cry.

It didn't take a genius to work out that she was worrying about something. It was worry that had made her irritable and bad tempered and it was the worry which was causing both the skin rash and the indigestion. When she had finished dressing I got her to sit down and then I asked her if anything in particular had been worrying her. 'Only my job,' she confessed. She shrugged as if I wouldn't really be interested but I persuaded her to tell me about it.

Look at this picture and try to imagine you are really there. Your body will respond not to reality but to your imagination, and you will shiver and feel cold

'I work for a small printing firm,' she told me at last. 'It's a family firm and last year I was promoted to an important administrative position. I'm very happy there and enjoy the job but there's a rumour going around that our firm is going to be taken over by a much bigger company.'

'And you don't like the idea of being caught up in the middle of a takeover?' I asked her to tell me exactly what was worrying her.

'I'm worried that if there is a take over I'll be made redundant,' she told me. 'When I got this job my husband and I bought a bigger house. Without my salary we won't be able to afford to pay the mortgage. If I lose my job we could lose our home.' As she told me this she started to cry. 'It's a beautiful house,' she told me. 'It had been neglected for years but we've spent every penny we could afford on it and now its wonderful. But if I lose this job everything we've worked for and everything we've done will be wasted...'

'Have you talked to anyone at work about the take over?' I asked her.

E dabbed her eyes with a tissue and shook her head. 'I don't even know whether or not there is definitely going to be a take over!'

'So, you're worrying about something that only **might** happen?'

E looked down at her lap. 'I know it sounds silly,' she admitted. 'But...,' she shrugged, 'the worst thing is not knowing what is going to happen.' She paused. 'The children would be devastated if we had to move,' she said. 'They've got good friends, they're at schools they like and they love the garden we've got.'

My advice to E was simple and straightforward.

I told her that she should talk to her boss and ask him to tell her the truth about the take over. 'And if there is going to be a take over,' I went on, 'ask your boss to tell you whether or not he thinks that the new firm will want to keep you on in the same position.'

I explained that her rash and her irritability were all being caused by the same thing: her imagination. Nothing had actually happened to make her ill but her fear of what **might** happen was quite enough to upset her and to cause genuine physical symptoms.

What was true for E is true for millions of others.

Like her lots of us suffer from very real symptoms of illness because our imaginations make us ill.

The human imagination is so powerful and so effective that it can fool your body. If you watch a television film with Arctic scenes it is quite likely that you will get up in the commercial break to make yourself a hot drink because your mind tells your body it is cold.

We worry about losing our jobs, being late, falling ill, losing the affection of the ones we love and a thousand and one other things. Our imagination gets the better of us and we worry endlessly (and often unjustifiably). As a result of our imaginary problems our health suffers in many different ways. All the symptoms and illnesses that can be caused by real problems can, just as easily, be caused by imaginary problems.

However, your imagination can also help to keep you well; if you know how to use it effectively you can use your imagination to help combat illness and to help protect you from mental and physical ill health.

By deliberately 'switching off' and replacing day to day worries with a peaceful memory or an entirely imaginary and tranquil scene you can combat the effects of stress on your body and overcome or avoid the damaging effects of too much anxiety. Try using my 'Daydreaming' technique. It isn't difficult to learn but it is an excellent way of staying alive and healthy in an increasingly stressful world where there is so much scope for your imagination to wreak havoc on your health and well being.

'RELAX YOUR MIND WITH A DAYDREAM'

Imagine. It is a warm, sunny day in early summer. There isn't a cloud in the sky and there is a soft, gentle, delicate breeze in the air which stops the heat from burning and the day from being oppressive.

It is a perfect day and for a few minutes you can forget all your fears, anxieties and worries. You are on a private island: alone, content and away from all everyday pressures and stresses; safe for now from the one thousand and one demands which normally make life difficult and which sometimes make it unbearable. You are alone but not lonely. Around you, the world is quiet but the silence is soothing. Occasionally, the breeze rustles the leaves in the nearby trees and in the distance you can hear insects in the grass, birds in the trees and the sound of the sea splashing onto the shore.

You are walking, slowly and effortlessly along a narrow country track. There are no cars, no people, no noises, no fumes and no rubbish on your island. You can take your time. You have all the time in the world.

On your left there is a hedgerow. On your right a lush, green meadow. At the base of the hedge there are primroses. In the meadow, early poppies are already unfolding their pink-red petals and dancing lightly in the whispering breeze. You are at peace with yourself and with the world in this private and lovely place.

You walk, on knowing that no one will ever find you or disturb you here. This is your personal world. No one else can come onto your island without your permission. No one can interrupt you or threaten you or make you sad while you are here. You know that, whatever happens elsewhere, you are safe here.

Slowly, your track begins to curve around to the left. There is a slight incline, too, and you realize that you are heading down towards the sea. Your island is a small one and you can see the sea all around you. It is a deep, beautiful blue and it stretches away, unspoilt and unmarked as far as you can see.

As you head down the track you gradually become aware of the fact that you can hear a stream nearby. You stop for a moment, move slightly to your left, and look through the hedge so that you can see the stream. It is quite shallow but the water runs fast and is

sparkling and crystal clear. The bed of the stream is made of small, pretty-looking stones though a few large rocks poke up above the surface of the water.

Further down, and closer to the seashore, the stream spreads out and becomes even shallower. Standing on the far side of the stream there are a dozen sturdy but old and gnarled trees. Beneath them, in the shade, there is a soft, inviting looking, mossy bank. You stand for a few more moments and stare at what seems to you to be the most beautiful and peaceful spot in the world. If you turn to your left you can see the stream, meandering down the gently sloping hillside of your island. If you turn to your right, you can see where the stream trickles down, between rocks and across a stretch of soft, golden sand, to the sea.

Using half a dozen large stepping stones you cross the stream, find a comfortable place to sit down on the mossy bank and rest your back against a tree.

It is like sitting in the most comfortable armchair ever designed. There is nowhere in the world quite so beautiful as your island and there is nowhere quite so peaceful as this spot where your island stream runs down into the sea. You rest, alone, content and silent. You feel comfortable, rested and happy.

When you close your eyes, you can hear the clear water of the stream gurgling and bubbling over its rocky bed. In the distance you can hear the sea crashing rhythmically and majestically onto the rocks. Above you, the breeze is rustling the leaves of the tree you are leaning up against.

You can feel the warmth of the sun filtering down through the leaves and your whole body feels relaxed. You love this peaceful spot.

You can stay here as long as you like. It is your island, your hideaway, your private escape from the real world. Here you can rest, untroubled by anxieties, stresses, pressures and worries.

And what makes this private place so very special is the fact that you can take it with you whenever you like and wherever you go. Your personal island will always be ready for you; will always welcome you and will always offer you peace and tranquillity. It never goes dark here. The sun never sets. It never goes cold. It never rains. This is your Camelot. This is your passport to peace, contentment and happiness.

MINI MIND GYM NO 1
ENJOY THE BEST DAYS OF YOUR LIFE – AGAIN

Every doctor in the world agrees that some physical exercise is an essential part of healthy life. But, although the brain can benefit from the right sort of exercise, most people ignore their minds – and don't give them the sort of exercise they so desperately need. Yet the right mental exercise can work wonders – and can help you conquer anxiety and stress.

If you replace unhappy feelings and miserable memories with good feelings and good memories, you can make yourself feel much better. Harvard psychologists have found that people who think about past experiences of loving and being loved raise their immunoglobulin levels and increase their bodies defences against infection and other diseases. By focusing on good memories and happy thoughts you can:

• **improve your physical health**
• **improve your mental strength**
• **improve your resistance to stress**
• **conquer sleeplessness**
• **improve your immunity to infections and other diseases**
• **achieve your ambitions and become more successful**

Try this mini mind gym exercise:
1. Find yourself a notebook and a pencil.
2. Go somewhere quiet – where you won't be disturbed by anyone.
3. Think back and decide which were the happiest days you have ever spent – the happiest days of your

life. Go right back into your childhood and search out secret, happy memories. Think of all the days in your adult life which have made you feel really good: holidays, days out, special birthdays, Christmas celebrations, exam successes, meeting someone you love, finding a new home, a reunion, the birth of a child, getting a new job etc. The more you think, the more really good days you will remember. Write down all the really good days you can think of. Find as many as you can.

4. Now choose your favourite seven – the seven best days of your life. And put them in a separate list: your all-time favourite week.

5. Look at the first day on your list and try to relive it. Try to experience the sounds and the smells and the conversations. Try to remember the weather, the buildings, the people – *everything*. Concentrate hard so that you feel as good as you did on the day itself. Try to remember the way you felt: the joy, the warmth, the happiness.

6. Do the same for the other six days on your list.

7. Now go back to your original, longer list and see if there are any days there that ought to be in your all-time favourite week. If you have difficulty in deciding which days to put in and which to drop out, you could extend your favourite week to ten days or even a fortnight.

Reliving good memories from your past should make you feel good – and should make the present feel better too. Keep your list of favourite days somewhere safe and try thinking through each day every time you feel sad or miserable. Try thinking through your favourite days first thing in the morning and last thing at night. Look at your list when you are feeling glum or downcast or when things seem to be going badly wrong. You will be astonished to see just how these uplifting memories can improve life for you.

Always remember that, however bad *today* may seem to be, there is always a chance that *tomorrow* may win a place in your all-time favourite week.

Note: if you really *cannot* remember any good days in your life then simply make some up. As long as you think happy, comforting, loving thoughts you can benefit just as much.

MINI MIND GYM No 2
LEARN TO TRUST YOUR
INSTINCTS AND INTUITION

Your mind is incredibly powerful. There is no computer in the world to match it, and yet the chances are that you have not yet tapped into its real power.

Most of us splutter along using just a tiny percentage of our natural skills – a bit like buying a Ferrari and using it to drive slowly to the local shops.

Some of your simplest, but hidden skills, could help you deal with many of your most threatening problems. For example: learn to trust your instincts.

Most people suppress, or are frightened to acknowledge, their own instinctive personal judgements. We have been taught to think carefully before making decisions and so we agonize over simple problems such as which shoes or tie to wear to work, which meal to choose on a restaurant menu.

Nowadays, we live in a world which is dominated by experts. We are taught to listen to them and to take their advice about everything. Yet most of the political, social, scientific and legal policies which turn out to be irrational, purposeless, vindictive, prejudiced or just plain stupid, were originally devised by experts.

Do not be afraid to stand by your feelings: never assume that the experts are right; don't be tricked or seduced into believing that the decisions made by society on your behalf are right or rational.

If you have the courage to learn to put yourself on automatic you will not only be able to use the hidden powers of your mind to make decisions for you but,

you will gradually acquire a strange sixth sense. Your natural, inborn sense of intuition will soon develop.

Look around and you will see that many apparently well-educated, seemingly sensible people, find it extraordinarily difficult to make simple decisions. Watch a diner in a restaurant trying to decide what to eat. Watch a man or woman in his or her bedroom trying to decide what to wear. Time and again you will see people creating stress and anxiety for themselves.

When faced with simple problems, learn to make up your mind to follow whatever thought springs first to the forefront. If your first instinct is to wear the blue shirt or dress then wear the blue and hang the consequences. If your first instinct is to choose the lasagne then choose the lasagne. Force yourself to think quickly and decisively. The chances are that your hidden intuitive powers will help you make the right decision immediately – without hours of agonizing. (If you doubt that I am right, just remember how many times you have spent ages making a decision – and then ended up with the clothes, meal or TV programme that your instincts told you was right an hour or so earlier!) You will liberate yourself from much unnecessary anxiety and if a decision proves to be misplaced you will free yourself from much damaging and destructive self-criticism. It is far less damaging to your self-confidence to be able to lay the blame on poor intuition rather

than to have to blame yourself for poor decision making.

By using your intuition to solve simple, day to day problems you will benefit in two ways. First, you will leave more time for conscious thought about decisions which really do matter. Second, you will hone your intuitive skills to a level where you can use your sub-conscious to help you find answers to the most difficult – and apparently insoluble – problems in your life.

Once your intuition is developed and you find yourself facing a genuinely difficult dicision you will hopefully have the courage to give up puzzling over it and allow your instincts to take over.

If you take a walk, sit in a warm, relaxing bath or sit down in front of the fire with a good book, your subconscious mind will continue to work on the problem – and to assess the various options. You will usually find that there is really only one solution. Gradually, you will be able to learn to trust your instincts in situations when the stakes are higher.

Learn to listen to your inner self and you will find peace and calm. Learn to say and do what you think is right, and to act in a way that makes you feel comfortable with yourself and your world. Do not allow yourself to be pressurized by the expectations or exhortations of society's experts.

MINI MIND GYM NO 3
RECAPTURE
YOUR TEENAGE DREAMS

You can overcome boredom and tiredness and put sparkle and enthusiasm back into your life by using your largely unused memory powers to take yourself back to when you were a teenager.

When we are young we all have many dreams. We fantasize a great deal about the future. We envisage ourselves conquering the world as musicians, sports stars or politicians, becoming great painters, writers or sculptors or travelling to distant places.

But society doesn't like dreamers: they are unproductive, they cause trouble and they do not fit neatly into the scheme of things. Society wants you to sell your soul for a small suburban house, a motor car and a barbecue in the back garden. Society needs workers and consumers, not dreamers.

The truth is, however, that you will be far more

likely to succeed, to survive, to combat stress and anxiety successfully and to be happy if you always hold your dreams close to your heart.

So ignore the people who want you to put aside and forget your dreams, ambitions and aspirations. If you allow your dreams to disappear then you will become sad, dull, aimless, miserable and vulnerable to stress. Keep your dreams close to you for as long as you live. Reach back into your memory, grab your teenage dreams and hold on to them.

More importantly, remember that a goal is nothing more than a dream with a deadline. Don't be afraid to give your dreams substance. Programme your dreams into your plans for the future. You don't have to realize your dreams, but you do have to keep them alive.

Think back to when you were a teenager and write down all the dreams you had. Then go down your list, cross out the ones that are totally, impossible, and think carefully about the rest . . .

MINI MIND GYM No 4
MEDITATION IS EASIER
THAN YOU THINK

Meditation is an excellent way to forget your worries, escape from the 'real world' and cleanse your mind of stress and anxiety.

Try this simple exercise for just 15 minutes a day – preferably, but not necessarily, at the same time of day so that it becomes a routine. You need to have a piece of paper and a pencil within reach.

1. Lie or sit down somewhere quiet and comfortable. If you are sitting down, choose a firm, upright chair. You should try to keep your back straight and deliberately relax your shoulder, back and neck muscles.

2. Pay attention to your stomach and watch it as you breathe in and breathe out. Look at nothing else. Try to keep your mind blank.

3. Whenever your mind wanders, or a thought or worry appears into your head, observe the thought as dispassionately as you can but do not allow it to disturb you. If the thought is an important one which you are frightened you will forget, write it down and then carry on as before – paying total attention to your breathing.

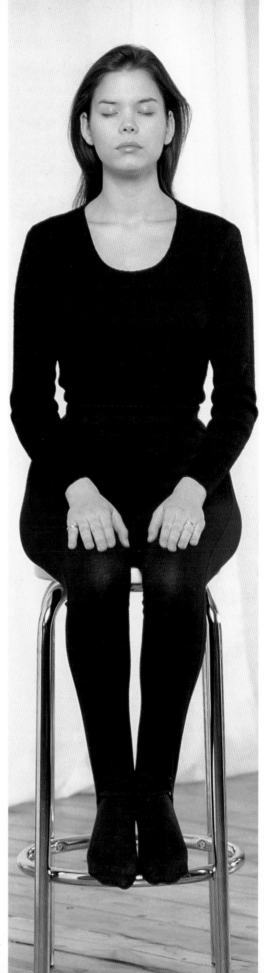

CHAPTER TEN

How You Can Use Exercise To Combat Stress

Stress, muscle tension and pain are interlinked, interdependent and inextricable. If you are under stress your muscles will be tense. If your muscles are tense they will be painful. The pain you get when you are under stress depends upon which muscles are tensed.

Indeed, the relationship between pain, stress and muscle tension works in other ways too. So, for example, if you are in pain because of a physical injury you will tense your muscles. As a result your susceptibility to stress will be increased.

"By stretching your muscles, exercise helps to remove accumulated tensions. As the tension goes, so the pain disappears too"

Exercise helps to break up these vicious circles in several ways:

• When you exercise you put aside your daily worries. By concentrating on what you are doing you force life's stresses to the back of your mind – and both your mind and your body benefit.

• By stretching your muscles, exercise helps to remove accumulated tensions. As the tension goes, so the pain disappears too.

• Many of the accumulated stresses in your body are a result of frustrations and disappointments and uncommitted anger. Modern life leads us into many situations where we want to explode – but where we know that losing our temper would be inappropriate or illegal. Your body's natural response to stress – which wants you to respond physically – leads to a build-up of muscle tension. The change in your muscles is designed to enable you to fight or to run away. But usually you do neither. When you exercise your body, you give yourself a chance to empty your muscles of those accumulated stresses and tensions.

• Regular exercise encourages your body to produce soothing and healing hormones called endorphins – your body's own version of the opiates. These hormones will help heal your ills and make you feel better.

• A sensible, regular exercise programme that improves your general health and fitness will increase your resistance to stress and reduce your susceptibility to stress-related illnesses.

• People who exercise regularly produce lower levels of a stress-related hormone called epinephrine (also known as adrenalin) and experience less dramatic blood pressure and heart rate rises during ordinary types of everyday stress. As a result, regular exercisers are far less likely to suffer from heart disease. At the same time, argue some experts, the production of a chemical called norepinephrine (also known as noradrenalin) increases dramatically during and after exercise and helps combat depression, increase happiness levels and tackle stress.

With all this evidence it is perhaps hardly surprising that today, more than eight out of ten doctors prescribe exercise for depressed or anxious patients.

'It's proving to be as important to mental health as nutrition and sleep are to physical health,' says a psychiatrist whose patients spend more time running round the track than they do lying on a couch.

There are three main ways in which you can exercise your body and liberate your mind: aerobic exercise, stretching and weight-lifting. Because each discipline offers its own advantages, I recommend that you use all three. To help you, I have prepared a stress-combatting exercise schedule which I call 'Trirobics'.

TRIROBICS DISCIPLINE 1: AEROBIC EXERCISE

Jogging, running, cycling and dancing (and specifically designed 'aerobic' exercises) all exercise your heart, and can help remove tensions from your inner body – especially your cardiovascular system. You should take part in aerobic exercise for a minimum of 20 minutes, three times a week. I suggest that you follow the simple aerobic exercise programme I have outlined on page 87. But beware; when aerobic exercise really became popular for the first time, thousands of people injured themselves. Joint, bone and muscle injuries were commonplace. If you take care and follow my advice carefully the risk of injury will be minimized.

• Do check with your doctor before you start an exercise programme.

• Do stop if you feel any pain.

• Do buy comfortable, well-fitting shoes. It doesn't matter very much what else you wear when you exercise – though large breasted women will undoubtedly feel far more comfortable if they wear good sports bras, and joggers should choose clothing that prevents chafing and that enables them to be seen in traffic – but good shoes which absorb some of the damaging impact incurred on landing, can dramatically reduce the risk of injury to feet, legs and spine.

TRIROBICS DISCIPLINE 2: STRETCHING

Stretching helps get rid of specific muscle tension and also helps by extending your range of joint movement. You should perform the simple stretching exercises such as those I have outlined on page 90 several times a week. You need spend only 30 seconds on each exercise, but do them regularly!

TRIROBICS DISCIPLINE 3: WEIGHT-LIFTING

When you lift weights you won't just increase the strength and power of your muscles – you will also increase the strength of your bones. Lifting weights will help improve your capacity to absorb stress into your muscles and will reduce your chances of developing stress-related aches and strains. (As a by-product it will also reduce your chances of suffering from weak bones or osteoporosis.) Follow the simple weight-lifting programme I have outlined on page 92 – remembering that the aim is not to build up enormous amounts of muscle bulk but to build up muscle strength. You don't have to look like a weight-lifter with massive, bulging muscles, to benefit from weight-lifting!

THE TRUTH ABOUT EXERCISE

Do you think you take enough exercise? The chances are high that you don't exercise enough.

You've probably meant to start exercising but have been too busy. Meanwhile, though you like to think you're fit, you know you aren't.

You may even worry that you're so unfit that taking up exercise could in fact do you more harm than good. There is some truth in that.

If you suddenly throw yourself into a hectic exercise programme, you could seriously injure yourself. But not doing any exercise is even worse.

Unless you exercise regularly, your health will be at risk and you will be more prone to disorders as varied as arthritis, osteoporosis, heart disease and depression.

Most of us live fairly sedentary lives. We travel in motor cars, buses and trains and we use gadgets and machines to help us cut down the workload in the house and garden. If you doubt me, just count the number of hours you spend sitting down each day.

However, your body *needs* exercise. In a few thousand years' time we may well have adapted to our sedentary existence, but, at the moment, your body is still designed for action. Many of the diseases which are most common today are partly caused by the fact that most of us do not exercise enough.

Here's a list of just some of the diseases that can be made worse by not doing any exercise and made better by a well-thought out exercise programme:

1. Arthritis: your joints need to keep moving or else they'll seize up.

2. Backache: sitting or standing in one position for long periods can result in strains that can cause long-term back trouble.

3. Headaches: without exercise, tension builds up in your muscles and pains in the head and neck develop as a result.

4. Anxiety: exercise is one of the best ways of getting rid of stress and tension that will otherwise build up.

5. Circulation problems: without exercise, the blood will stagnate in your veins and the result will be that you will be more likely to suffer from cold hands, cold feet and varicose veins.

6. Depression: regular exercise can help you avoid or fight depression.

7. Heart trouble: without exercise your heart will become weak and flabby – and the slightest exertion will put it under strain. A well-thought out exercise programme will improve the power and strength of your heart.

8. Digestive upsets: indigestion, irritable bowel syndrome and many other digestive problems are caused by sitting around too much.

9. Obesity: your weight is a result of the amount of food you eat and the amount you burn up through exercise; the more exercise you do, the more food you'll burn up – and the slimmer you'll get. More important still, if you exercise regularly your muscle tone will improve and you'll look and feel slimmer and healthier.

10. Sleeplessness: regular exercise will help you sleep better without pills.

So, how much exercise should you do and what should you do?

The first thing you must do is check with your doctor if you are in any doubt about your fitness to undertake an exercise programme.

Don't just rush down to your gym and start lifting the heaviest weights you can find or pedalling the exercise bicycle as fast as it will go – you'll almost certainly make yourself ill if you do. And you could kill yourself.

Try to find a gym with a good coach, a well-run aerobics class or a sports club that you can join.

A good coach is vital: he or she will show you how to take your pulse before and after every exercise session. Within a few weeks you should notice that your pulse will go back to its normal rate quicker and quicker after exercising. You should also notice that your normal pulse rate gets lower as you get fitter.

One of the by-products of taking up an exercise programme is that you'll meet new friends with whom you can share the trials and tribulations of getting fit. You'll do better and get more out of your exercise programme if it is fun so try to choose a type of exercise that you think you'll enjoy.

Allocate time for exercise and stick to it. If you decide to exercise only when you've got free time you'll never do anything. You need to set aside time for a properly organized exercise programme. But it need not be much. Three sessions a week is plenty. You should allow a full hour for each session though to start with you probably won't be able to manage that much. If you are really pushed for time you can squeeze a useful exercise programme into three 20 minute slots. Can there be anyone who can't manage one hour a week?

THE PERILS OF TRYING (TOO HARD) TO GET FIT

BEWARE: EXERCISE CAN BE DANGEROUS – PARTICULARLY IF YOU START A NEW EXERCISE PROGRAMME WITHOUT CAREFUL PLANNING AND WITHOUT THINKING ABOUT THE HAZARDS. A BADLY ORGANIZED EXERCISE PROGRAMME CAN DO FAR MORE HARM THAN GOOD AND CAN PRODUCE AN ENORMOUS VARIETY OF PHYSICAL PROBLEMS – INEVITABLY RAISING, RATHER THAN REDUCING, STRESS LEVELS. BELOW ARE SOME OF THE PROBLEMS YOU COULD FACE.

HEART THE NUMBER OF YOUNG – AND APPARENTLY FIT – SPORTSMEN WHO COLLAPSE AND HAVE HEART ATTACKS IS HORRIFYINGLY HIGH. THE OLDER YOU ARE – AND THE MORE UNFIT – THE GREATER YOUR CHANCES OF CAUSING SERIOUS AND POSSIBLY PERMANENT DAMAGE TO YOUR HEART BY OVER-EXERCISING. YOU *MUST* BEGIN YOUR EXERCISE PROGRAMME SLOWLY.

HIP JOINT TOO MUCH EXERCISE CAN WEAR OUT THE HIP JOINT PREMATURELY. HURDLERS – WHO PUT A GREATER THAN AVERAGE STRAIN ON THEIR HIP JOINTS – EXPECT TO SUFFER FROM PREMATURE DEGENERATIVE JOINT DISEASE OF THE HIP.

EYES A SQUASH BALL IN THE EYE CAN DO AN ENORMOUS AMOUNT OF DAMAGE.

BREASTS WOMEN WHO EXERCISE REGULARLY CAN SUFFER FROM BREAST SAG. WEARING STRONG 'ATHLETIC' SUPPORT BRAS WILL ONLY PARTLY PREVENT THIS. CONSTANT RUBBING OF THE NIPPLES – IN BOTH MEN AND WOMEN – CAN CAUSE SORENESS AND BLEEDING. SPECIAL CREAMS AND NIPPLE SHIELDS CAN BE BOUGHT TO HELP.

STOMACH DISORDERS ROUGHLY 10 PER CENT OF RUNNERS AND JOGGERS SUFFER FROM HEARTBURN, AND 25 PER CENT SUFFER FROM ABDOMINAL CRAMP OR DIARRHOEA DURING OR AFTER A COMPETITIVE RUN.

GROIN WOMEN WHO EXERCISE TOO MUCH MAY COMPLAIN OF IRREGULAR PERIODS AND LOW FERTILITY LEVELS. MEN WHO EXERCISE REGULARLY HAVE 30 PER CENT LESS MALE HORMONES THAN MEN WHO DON'T – THIS MAY AFFECT THEIR SEX LIVES.

ELBOWS TENNIS ELBOW
IS A PAINFUL DISORDER
WHICH CAN BE EXTREMELY
DIFFICULT TO TREAT. IT IS
CAUSED BY OVERUSE OF THE
ELBOW JOINT.

NECK DAMAGE TO THE
CERVICAL SPINE – WITH
POSSIBLE PARALYSIS – CAN
HAPPEN IN COMBAT SPORTS.

SHOULDERS SHOULDER
PROBLEMS ARE COMMON PLACE
AMONG TENNIS, BADMINTON
AND GOLF PLAYERS.

LUNGS EXERCISE-INDUCED
ASTHMA IS COMMON AND MAY
AFFECT THOSE WHO HAVE A
HISTORY OF CHILDHOOD
ASTHMA OR WHEEZY
BRONCHITIS, PATIENTS WITH
ECZEMA OR HAY FEVER AND
EVEN THOSE WHO ARE RELATED
TO ASTHMA SUFFERERS.
EXERCISE OUT DOORS IN LARGE
POLLUTED CITIES INCREASE
THEIR RISK OF CHEST
INFECTIONS.

KNEES THE KNEE IS THE
MOST DELICATE AND MOST
INJURY-PRONE OF ALL JOINTS.
KNEE INJURIES ARE COMMON
AMONG REGULAR EXERCISERS.
THE MOST DANGEROUS INJURIES
INVOLVE THE LIGAMENTS.

INFECTION SOME EXPERTS
BELIEVE THAT TOO MUCH,
OVER-ENTHUSIASTIC EXERCISE
'WEARS OUT' THE BODY'S
DEFENCES AND MAKES IT
VULNERABLE TO INFECTION.

BACKACHE THE BACK
CONSISTS OF SCORES OF
SEPARATE JOINTS WHICH ARE
JIGGLED AND JOGGLED BY
REPETITIVE EXERCISE.

KIDNEYS TOO MUCH
EXERCISE CAN PUT THE
KIDNEYS UNDER CONSTANT HIGH
PRESSURE – RESULTING IN A
CONDITION KNOWN AS ATHLETIC
PSEUDONEPHRITIS.

LOWER LEG INJURIES OF THE
LOWER LEG AFFECTING THOSE
PEOPLE WHO EXERCISE
FREQUENTLY INCLUDE: STRESS
FRACTURES, SHIN SPLINTS,
RUPTURED ACHILLES TENDON,
MUSCLE STRAINS AND
CALCANEAL BURSA.

FEET ATHLETES FOOT AND
BLISTERS ARE COMMON
DISORDERS. BUT ARTHRITIS,
FRACTURES AND PROBLEMS
SUCH AS CALCANEAL SPURS
CAN MAKE EVEN WALKING
DIFFICULT FOR THE OVER-
ENTHUSIASTIC ATHLETE.

Try to make your exercise time inviolable and give it priority over other, less vital tasks.

You don't need a lot of money to take up exercise but do buy the right gear – the best you can afford. Remember: you're not trying to look fashionable, but you do need shoes that are comfortable and give good support and since you'll be sweating a lot when you start exercising properly, you'll need clothes that can be washed often, quickly and easily.

Finally, remember the most important rule for exercise: it should never hurt. Pain is your body's way of saying 'stop'. If you ignore a pain – and attempt to blunder bravely through the pain barrier – you will almost certainly injure yourself.

JOIN A GYM!

It is perfectly possible to get all the exercise you need in order to improve your physical fitness and help your mind conquer stress without ever going anywhere near a gym. But if there is a local gym, I suggest that you join it! You'll benefit in several ways.

They are bound to have a wider range of equipment than you will want to buy for yourself; good gyms are staffed with well-qualified instructors who can help you develop an exercise programme to suit your own personal needs. And you'll find, too, that most gyms are friendly places. You will benefit enormously from the support and companionship of those around you. It is much more fun to exercise in a group than it is to exercise alone.

THE HAZARDS OF RUNNING

One of the biggest hazards that runners face is traffic. Every year in America around 8,000 runners are killed by cars – and another 100,000 are injured. Although there are no accurate figures for the U.K., the figures here are probably just as shocking. Runners should keep well away from traffic – and make sure that they wear fluorescent clothing if they go out running in the dark.

THE HEART Runners as young as 18 years old have died of heart attacks. On average, at least one runner has a heart attack during a big marathon and runners – being less fit than marathon runners – are probably

more at risk. Always stop running if you get any pain, palpitations or breathlessness.

THE CHEST It isn't just women who get sore nipples – men suffer too. Runners are advised to put cream on their nipples to stop them bleeding or getting sore.

THE LUNGS Breathing in car exhaust fumes will do your lungs no good at all. In fact runners who get their exercise in the city are doing themselves as much damage as if they smoked a pack of 20 cigarettes a day.

THE BACK Runners who exercise for too long on hard surfaces are particularly likely to suffer from backache. Every one hour's running means that the back gets 10,000 vibrations it doesn't want. Running on cambered roads means that the strains on the back are particularly bad because one leg is always running lower than the other.

THE STOMACH Runners who train for too long are likely to suffer from intestinal complaints as varied as diarrhoea and indigestion.

THE GROIN Men who run regularly have 30 per cent less male hormones than men who do not. If the weather is bad men run the risk of getting penile frost bite – which is as nasty as it sounds.

THE HIPS Too much running, especially on hard surfaces, can cause arthritis in the hips.

THE KNEE The knee is the joint that gives all sportsmen most trouble. Runners face muscle, cartilage and ligament injuries if they over-train.

THE THIGHS Hamstrings are easily pulled – and can take weeks to recover. Part-time runners who only go out onto the roads occasionally are much more at risk than regulars.

THE FEET Hard roads can mean that blisters develop or that bleeding beneath the nails turns them black.

THE KIDNEYS Runners who do too much, can develop a long-term kidney problem – thought to be caused by all the vibrations the body has to endure.

THE ANKLES Sprains and strains can occur when runners are tired or run on rough ground.

TEN REASONS WHY A CAREFULLY PREPARED RUNNING PROGRAMME IS GOOD FOR YOU (APART FROM HELPING YOU DEAL WITH STRESS) AND HOW IT CAN HELP YOUR HEALTH:

1. RUNNING WILL HELP KEEP YOUR JOINTS LUBRICATED AND SUPPLE AND WILL HELP PREVENT ARTHRITIS IN LATER LIFE.

2. *REGULAR EXERCISE WILL IMPROVE THE POWER AND STRENGTH OF YOUR HEART, AND REDUCE YOUR CHANCES OF HAVING A HEART ATTACK. RUNNING IS A PRACTICAL WAY TO GET THE EXERCISE YOU NEED.*

3. IF YOU ARE OVERWEIGHT YOU CAN BURN UP UNWANTED CALORIES, AND THUS LOSE WEIGHT, BY RUNNING REGULARLY.

4. *MUSCLE TONE AND MUSCLE POWER WILL IMPROVE WITH REGULAR EXERCISE AND YOU WILL BE LESS LIKELY TO SUFFER FROM CRAMPS OR OTHER PROBLEMS.*

5. IF YOU SUFFER FROM INDIGESTION, HEARTBURN OR ANY SIMILAR PROBLEMS THEN REGULAR EXERCISE *CAN* HELP TO SETTLE YOUR STOMACH AND PROTECT YOU FROM FUTURE TROUBLE. BY HELPING TO REDUCE YOUR STRESS LEVELS, RUNNING COULD HELP PREVENT THE DEVELOPMENT OF AN ULCER.

6. *RUNNING WILL HELP YOUR BREATHING. IN ORDER TO RUN PROPERLY, YOU HAVE TO LEARN TO BREATHE WELL.*

7. RUNNING OUT OF DOORS WILL HELP IMPROVE THE CONDITION OF YOUR SKIN. TOO MUCH TIME SPENT INDOORS LEADS TO DRYNESS AND INCREASES THE RISK OF SKIN PROBLEMS SUCH AS ECZEMA AND DERMATITIS.

8. *RUNNING WILL HELP IMPROVE YOUR CIRCULATION – AND REDUCE YOUR CHANCES OF SUFFERING FROM VARICOSE VEINS, PILES AND COLD HANDS.*

9. IF YOUR JOB IS BORING OR UNSATISFYING YOU WILL BE ABLE TO OBTAIN MUCH PERSONAL SATISFACTION AND PLEASURE, BOTH FROM WATCHING YOUR FITNESS LEVELS IMPROVE, AND FROM RUNNING WITH NEW FRIENDS.

10. *RUNNING REGULARLY WILL IMPROVE YOUR GENERAL HEALTH AND REDUCE YOUR SUSCEPTIBILITY TO A WIDE VARIETY OF ILLNESSES AND INFECTIONS.*

WARNING

1. DO NOT START AN EXERCISE PROGRAMME
UNTIL YOU HAVE CHECKED WITH YOUR DOCTOR
THAT THE PROGRAMME IS SUITABLE FOR YOU.
MAKE SURE THAT YOU TELL HIM ABOUT ANY
TREATMENT YOU ARE RECEIVING AND ABOUT
ANY SYMPTOMS FROM WHICH YOU SUFFER.

2. YOU MUST STOP EXERCISING IF YOU FEEL
FAINT, DIZZY, BREATHLESS OR NAUSEATED OR
IF YOU NOTICE ANY PAIN OR FEEL UNWELL IN
ANY WAY. **G**ET EXPERT HELP IMMEDIATELY
AND DO NOT START EXERCISING AGAIN UNTIL
YOU HAVE BEEN GIVEN THE 'ALL CLEAR' BY
YOUR DOCTOR

EXERCISE GETS RID OF ANGER

Research at the University of California, in the U.S.A., has shown that people who exercise regularly don't just get fitter but also get rid of anger and aggression that might otherwise build up inside them.

Accumulated anger is a major cause of stress-illnesses.

TRIROBICS

A good exercise programme should be fun and varied. It should be hard work but never painful.

Many modern exercise programmes have been designed to be used by people who have plenty of time and energy and a burning desire to become superfit athletes.

Trirobics is different – it is a truly holistic exercise programme. It is specially designed to suit the reader of this book who wants to try a simple, relatively undemanding, easy-to-understand, exercise programme.

Trirobics is designed for the individual who wants to get fit without getting up at 6.00 a.m. to go jogging in the rain. It does not require a high level of starting fitness but does offer you an effective way of combating stress, reducing muscle tension, increasing general fitness and strength and improving your health without crippling you or turning you into an exercise junkie.

As I have already explained, Trirobics consists of three parts: aerobics – to improve the condition of your heart and your general level of fitness; stretching – to timprove your flexibility and suppleness and weight-training – to improve your muscle and bone strength.

HOW TO TAKE YOUR PULSE

Hold the tips of your left forefinger and middle finger on the artery in your wrist.

THE TRIROBICS PROGRAMME

To develop and maintain your stress resistance, general endurance, cardiovascular fitness and muscular strength you should do the following:

- **C**ONSULT YOUR DOCTOR *BEFORE* YOU BEGIN THE **T**RIROBICS PROGRAMME AND ASK FOR A CHECKUP.
- *T*RAIN A MINIMUM OF THREE AND A MAXIMUM OF FIVE TIMES A WEEK.
- **T**RAIN FOR BETWEEN **20** AND **60** MINUTES AT A TIME.
- *A*IM AT A MINIMUM OF **60** MINUTES SOLID *T*RIROBICS TRAINING EVERY WEEK.
- **N**EVER DO MORE THAN FIVE HOURS' **T**RIROBICS TRAINING IN ANY ONE WEEK.
- *E*NSURE WHEN POSSIBLE THAT EACH TRAINING SESSION INCLUDES ELEMENTS FROM EACH BRANCH OF *T*RIROBICS.
- **W**ARM UP CAREFULLY *BEFORE* EVERY **T**RIROBICS SESSION.
- *C*OOL DOWN CAREFULLY AFTER EVERY *T*RIROBICS SESSION.
- **A**VOID ANYTHING THAT YOU FIND PAINFUL OR THAT YOU DO NOT ENJOY.
- *S*TOP IMMEDIATELY IF YOU SUFFER FROM PAIN, BREATHLESSNESS, FEEL DIZZY OR NOTICE ANY OTHER SYMPTOMS.
- **V**ARY YOUR EXERCISE PROGRAMME CONSTANTLY IN ORDER TO MAINTAIN YOUR INTEREST AND TO MAXIMIZE YOUR GENERAL FITNESS LEVEL.
- *C*ONTINUE TO TRAIN REGULARLY EVEN WHEN YOU FEEL FIT AND STRESS FREE.
- **D**URING THE AEROBIC SEGMENT OF THE **T**RIROBICS PROGRAMME YOU SHOULD AIM TO GET (AND KEEP) YOUR PULSE RATE IN THE RANGE SHOWN OVERLEAF:

Age	Pulse Range
15-19	120-180
20-24	115-175
25-29	115-170
30-34	110-165
35-39	105-160
40-44	105-155
45-49	100-150
50-54	95-145
55-59	95-140
60-64	90-135
65-69	90-135
70-74	80-130
75+	80-125

TRIROBICS – THE ENDURANCE PROGRAMME

Who do you think is fittest? A 25-year-old man who works on the trapeze in a circus and who spends several hours a day hurling himself through the air and bending himself into unlikely looking positions; a 25-year-old man who spends one hour a day in the gym lifting weights and who has impressively clear cut musculature; or a 25-year-old man who never goes into a gym and never deliberately takes any exercise but cycles three miles to and from work every day?

All things being equal the man who cycles to work will be by far the fittest and healthiest of the three – and also the one most likely to be able to combat physical and mental illness successfully.

Fitness – the capacity to do hard physical work without slowing down, weakening or getting tired – depends upon the condition of the *whole* body: the heart, the lungs and the muscles. It has nothing to do with pure muscle strength or agility.

Any human activity needs energy and your body gets its energy from food. But food by itself isn't enough – your body also needs oxygen to help burn up the food and to turn it into energy.

Your body can store food but it can't store oxygen, so when you are exercising, your fitness level – your ability to cope with enhanced demands or emergencies – depends upon your body's ability to draw in oxygen quickly enough to supply your muscles, organs and tissues when they are under pressure. Your lungs have to bring the oxygen in, your heart has to pump the blood containing the oxygen around your arteries and your arterial and capillary system has to be well-developed so that the oxygen can get to the cells which need it as quickly as possible.

When you're resting, your body won't have much difficulty in pulling enough oxygen. But if you are unfit, as soon as you start to run or do anything physically demanding you will get breathless, you will start noticing all sorts of uncomfortable aches and pains and you will fall down exhausted, relatively quickly.

At this stage you may argue that you don't need to be fit because you spend most of your time sitting down at a desk, sitting in your car or slumped down in front of the TV set.

But you do need to be fit because your body was designed to be used and if it isn't used regularly, then it will quickly start to deteriorate: your lungs won't work as efficiently, your heart will grow weak and flabby, your muscles will become weak and your circulatory system will stop working as well as it could. Your body's ability to deliver oxygen to the organs and muscles which need it will deteriorate and your body's capacity to cope with physical or mental emergencies will be dramatically reduced.

Remember it isn't only physical dangers which put demands on your body. Mental problems – stresses and anxieties – also put demands on your body and if you are physically unfit then a little bit of stress will make you feel tired and ill, and a lot of stress could seriously damage or even kill you.

The good news is that, however unfit you have allowed yourself to become, you can restore your body to physical fitness and build up your endurance by following the correct exercise programme (though, of course, you should see your doctor and get his permission before you start any exercise programme at all).

The sort of exercises that make up the endurance

segment of the Trirobics training programme have been chosen because they will help to improve the strength and efficiency of your heart, will increase the size and number of blood vessels capable of carrying oxygen around your body, will improve the tone of your muscles, will increase the efficiency of your lungs and will, in general, increase the efficiency of your body's oxygen supply system. In addition, as a bonus, you will find yourself better able to relax, better able to deal with stress, better able to sleep and better able to work hard without getting tired. You'll probably also feel more self-confident and more self-assured as you get fitter and stronger.

You will notice that the list of recommended exercises in the endurance programme does not include things like isometrics (deliberately contracting muscles without producing movement) or calisthenics (exercises such as touching your toes which depend upon flexibility, or press-ups which depend upon existing muscle strength). These exercises are useful – either for loosening up muscles and easing stiff joints, or for maintaining muscle tone and strength but they do not help build up endurance.

Nor do short or undemanding exercises help build up your endurance.

If you get your exercise in short sprints you will get out of breath quickly – creating an oxygen need that your heart and lungs cannot possibly satisfy without forcing you to slow down and rest. If you get your exercise in gentle five-minute walks, you will never put your body under any pressure – and you will not improve your endurance fitness.

To build up your body's endurance capacity you must exercise regularly and consistently in such a way that your lungs and heart have to start working more efficiency and more effectively in order to get oxygen supplies to your tissues.

But you must not over do it. If you do too much endurance training there is a risk that you will put an excessive strain on your heart or that you will damage your joints. When jogging first became popular a few years, ago many enthusiasts spent hours pounding the streets and ended up in hospital complaining of backache and hip, knee, ankle and foot problems.

The aim of the endurance programme is to improve your general fitness levels – not to turn you into a physical wreck. This programme is designed to help you get fitter and stronger – so that you can cope more effectively with physical and mental stresses. The endurance programme is not designed to turn you into a medal winning athlete. Medal winning requires a level of persistence and determination that must inevitably put your health at risk.

In order to build up your endurance levels the exercise you choose must demand oxygen and must result in an increase in your heart rate. If your heart rate goes up to around 150 beats a minute (or to the upper end of the recommended endurance range for your age) then your body will begin to benefit quite quickly – after about five minutes of exercise. If your heart rate doesn't go up quite that far then you can still benefit but you will have to exercise for longer.

So much for theory. Here are the practical steps which you must follow to build up your endurance levels and to increase your resistance to stress:

1. You must undertake endurance exercise at least twice a week and no more than five times a week. Three times a week is ideal. It is best if you have a day's rest between exercise sessions.

2. Each endurance exercise segment should last for at least ten minutes. If your exercise segment is short then you should be sweaty and slightly breathless by the time you have finished.

3. You can build up your own endurance exercise programme by studying the Endurance Choice Table which shows the value of different types of exercise. Aim to score a minimum of 70 points every week – and try to build up to 100 points. To make things as simple as possible try to measure out (using a motor car or bicycle odometer) precise distances – e.g. 1, 2, or 3 miles.

4. Before starting an endurance exercise, you must warm up your muscles and loosen your joints by exercising gently, and remember it is important to cool down afterwards. You will benefit most if you perform warm-up exercises that match the endurance exercise you are about to begin. For example, if you are about to start running then warm up by walking and then, when you have finished, cool down by walking again.

ENDURANCE CHOICE TABLE

1. RUNNING (OUT OF DOORS ON A FLAT COURSE OR ON A RUNNING MACHINE):

1 mile in 20 minutes or less: 3 points

1 mile in 15 minutes or less: 6 points

1 mile in 12 minutes or less: 9 points

1 mile in 10 minutes or less: 12 points

1 mile in 8 minutes or less: 15 points

If you run for longer than 1 mile, work out your points from your time. So, if you cover 2 miles in 20 minutes you get 24 points (for example, 2 x 1 mile at 10 minutes per mile or 1 x 1 mile at 8 minutes per mile and 1 x 1 mile at 12 minutes per mile).

Note: if you are too tired to keep running don't be afraid to stop and walk. You can 'mix and match' walking and running and still collect points.

2. WALKING (ON THE FLAT):

1 mile in 20 minutes or less: 3 points (no points if walking slower than 3 mph unless you walk for more than an hour – e.g. playing golf – in which case you can score 5 points an hour)

3. SWIMMING:

600 yards in 15 minutes or less: 15 points

4. CYCLING (ON THE FLAT)

a) racing bike:

2 miles in 12 minutes or less: 3 points

2 miles in 8 minutes or less: 6 points

2 miles in 6 minutes or less: 9 points

b) mountain bike:

2 miles in 20 minutes or less: 3 points

2 miles in 14 minutes or less: 6 points

2 miles in 10 minutes or less: 9 points

5. SKIPPING:

10 minutes skipping: 10 points

6. AEROBICS CLASS:

a) Beginners' class:

60 minutes: 8 points

b) Intermediate class:

60 minutes: 10 points

c) Advanced class:

60 minutes: 15 points

7. SQUASH, TENNIS, FOOTBALL, RUGBY, BASKETBALL ETC. (assumes more or less continuous exercise – no time allowed for breaks etc.):

60 minutes play: 15 points

TRIROBICS – THE FLEXIBILITY PROGRAMME

Flexibility is a major component of the trirobics programme. If you are too stiff you will not only find movement and exercise difficult, or even painful, but you will also dramatically increase your chances of suffering from injury, muscular pain and postural problems such as backache.

If you spend all day at a desk your back muscles will stretch, your chest muscles will shorten and you will become permanently round shouldered.

Women who wear high-heeled shoes develop shortened Achilles' tendons at the back of the ankle. When walking or running in flat shoes, they tend to suffer from strained tendons.

Too much sitting results in shortening of the muscles on the back of the thighs – the hamstrings. Many cases of backache are caused by the fact that tight hamstrings can tilt the pelvis forwards and push the vertebra in the lower spine out of line.

A few minutes a week spent stretching will improve your performance during the endurance exercise programme, improve your posture and general health and reduce your chances of suffering from a wide range of muscle and joint injuries. Many people find that stretching exercises are mentally as well as physically soothing. Do remember, however, that stretching is not a suitable alternative to warm-up exercises.

The simple flexibility-enhancing exercises described here should be performed gently and carefully. Do not do anything that hurts you. And do not 'bounce' in an attempt to improve your reach. You will only benefit if you stretch slowly and gradually – and then hold the stretched position for a few moments.

If you enjoy a particular sport – golf, running, tennis, for example – devise your own stretching exercises that will aid the muscles and joints that *you* use. Golfers, for example, need a considerable amount of body and neck flexibility while runners need flexible shoulder muscles as well as flexible hamstring muscles.

1. TO INCREASE THE FLEXIBILITY OF YOUR LOWER BACK AND HAMSTRING MUSCLES:

SIT ON THE FLOOR WITH YOUR LEGS STRAIGHT, YOUR KNEES LOCKED AND YOUR FEET TOUCHING A WALL. REST YOUR HANDS ON YOUR KNEES.

SLOWLY BEND FORWARDS AND TRY TO TOUCH THE WALL. WHEN YOU HAVE REACHED AS FAR FORWARDS AS YOU CAN HOLD THE POSITION WHILE YOU COUNT TO FIVE.

SIT BACK. RELAX WHILE YOU COUNT TO FIVE AND THEN REPEAT THE EXERCISE UP TO FIVE TIMES IF YOU CAN.

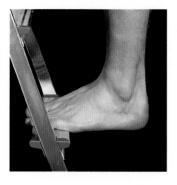
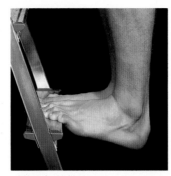
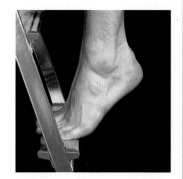

2. TO INCREASE THE FLEXIBILITY OF YOUR ACHILLES' TENDONS AND CALF MUSCLES:

STAND WITH YOUR TOES ON THE EDGE OF A STEP AND YOUR HEELS HANGING OVER THE EDGE. LOWER YOUR HEELS SO THAT THEY ARE BELOW YOUR TOES. HOLD THIS POSITION WHILE YOU COUNT TO FIVE. THEN LIFT YOURSELF UPWARDS AND REST FOR A COUNT OF FIVE. REPEAT THE EXERCISE UP TO FIVE TIMES IF YOU CAN.

TRIROBICS – THE STRENGTH PROGRAMME

It used to be thought that weight-lifting was of negligible health value – and of use only to individuals who wanted huge muscles.

However, although it is true that weight-lifting alone is of limited value – in a way it is like adding to the size of the bodywork of a motor car without making any modifications to the engine – it is now known that weight-lifting does have some previously unexpected value, for, in addition to improving muscle size and strength, a regular weight-lifting programme can improve the strength of bones – thereby reducing the risk of fractures and providing a considerable amount of protection against diseases such as osteoporosis.

Even elderly people can benefit from weight-training exercises. A study in Boston, U.S.A. showed that after eight weeks of exercise, ten frail 90 year olds almost doubled their muscle strength, and substantially improved their mobility. Since muscle weakness is a contributory factor in many falls among the elderly, weight-training could clearly prevent many potentially fatal accidents.

STRENGTH ENHANCEMENT PROGRAMME

Most towns – even small ones – have well-equipped gyms where you can, under supervision, learn how to use equipment designed to help you improve the strength of all your muscles.

My advice is that you should join a gym, or visit one regularly, and begin a varied, but regular, exercise programme. Exercises should be repeated ('reps') until your muscles feel tired – though *not* through or past the point of pain.

If you cannot join a gym, the alternative is to buy a pair of dumb-bells. Seek advice from a skilled specialist on the best weight to use. You can use these to help you exercise and strengthen most of your muscles. When performing these exercises keep your head and body as still as you can. And, remember – do not do anything that hurts! When you are holding the dumb-bells above your head or body make sure that you stop the exercise *before* you are too tired to lower the weights safely.

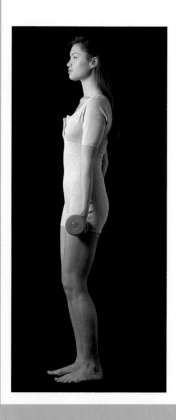

1. TO DEVELOP THE MUSCLES AT THE FRONT OF YOUR UPPER ARMS:

STAND WITH YOUR FEET SLIGHTLY APART AND YOUR KNEES SLIGHTLY BENT HOLDING A DUMB-BELL IN EACH HAND.

USING ONLY YOUR ARM MUSCLES, LIFT THE RIGHT DUMB-BELL UP TO YOUR SHOULDER. THEN SLOWLY LOWER IT. REPEAT THE EXERCISE WITH THE LEFT ARM.

2. TO DEVELOP THE MUSCLES OF YOUR SHOULDERS AND UPPER BACK:

LIE DOWN ON YOUR TUMMY WITH YOUR ARMS STRETCHED OUT SIDEWAYS AND HORIZONTALLY. YOU SHOULD BE HOLDING YOUR DUMB-BELLS WITH YOUR PALMS FACING THE FLOOR.

THEN, RAISE YOUR ARMS UPWARDS AS HIGH AS YOU CAN – AND LOWER THEM AGAIN. REPEAT THE EXERCISE.

3. TO DEVELOP YOUR SHOULDER MUSCLES:

A) LIE FLAT ON YOUR BACK WITH YOUR ARMS STRETCHED OUT BEHIND YOUR HEAD. YOUR ELBOW SHOULD BE BENT AT RIGHT ANGLES AND YOUR FOREARMS SHOULD BE PARALLEL TO YOUR BODY. YOUR PALMS SHOULD BE FACING UPWARDS.

LIFT THE DUMB-BELL IN YOUR RIGHT HAND AND MOVE IT SO THAT IT IS RESTING ON THE FLOOR BY YOUR WAIST. KEEP YOUR UPPER ARM AND ELBOW IN CONTACT WITH THE FLOOR. MOVE YOUR RIGHT ARM BACK TO THE STARTING POINT AND THEN DO THE SAME EXERCISE WITH YOUR LEFT ARM.

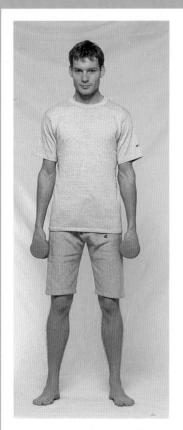

B) *Stand with your feet apart and your knees slightly bent. Your hands, holding your dumb-bells, should be by your sides and facing inwards. Then, moving both arms at once, lift your hands sideways until your arms are horizontal to the ground. Lower and then repeat the exercise.*

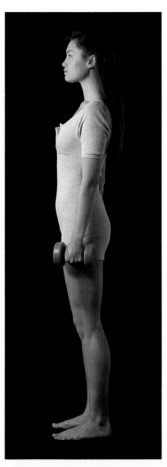

C) *Stand with your feet apart and your knees slightly bent. Your hands, holding your dumb-bells should be by your sides and facing inwards. Then, moving both arms at once lift your hands forwards until your arms are horizontal to the ground. Lower and then repeat the exercise.*

d) STAND WITH YOUR FEET APART AND YOUR KNEES SLIGHTLY BENT. YOUR HANDS, HOLDING YOUR DUMB-BELLS SHOULD BE BY YOUR SIDES AND FACING BACKWARDS. THEN, MOVING BOTH ARMS AT ONCE LIFT YOUR HANDS BACKWARDS AS HIGH AS YOU CAN WITHOUT BENDING YOUR BODY. LOWER AND THEN REPEAT THE EXERCISE.

WARNING

IF YOU ATTEND AN AEROBICS CLASS MAKE SURE THAT IT IS 'LOW-IMPACT AEROBICS' RATHER THAN 'HIGH-IMPACT AEROBICS'. THE DIFFERENCE IS SIMPLE.

IN 'LOW-IMPACT AEROBICS' YOU ALWAYS KEEP ONE FOOT ON THE GROUND WHEREAS IN 'HIGH-IMPACT AEROBICS' THERE IS A LOT OF JUMPING AND LEAPING ABOUT WITH BOTH FEET IN THE AIR – AND AN INEVITABLE HEAVY IMPACT WHEN YOU LAND ON THE GROUND.

THEREFORE THE RISK OF DEVELOPING A STRESS FRACTURE OR INJURING YOURSELF IN SOME OTHER WAY IS MUCH HIGHER. ONE SURVEY OF 28 FITNESS CENTRES SHOWED THAT ONE IN TWO PEOPLE WHO ATTEND 'HIGH-IMPACT AEROBICS' CLASSES INJURE THEMSELVES.

YOU CAN BUILD UP YOUR ENDURANCE LEVELS JUST AS WELL WITH 'LOW-IMPACT AEROBICS' AS WITH 'HIGH-IMPACT AEROBICS'.

4. TO DEVELOP THE MUSCLES OF YOUR SHOULDER AND BACK:

LIE ON YOUR BACK WITH YOUR ARMS STRETCHED OUT SIDEWAYS AND HORIZONTALLY. HOLD YOUR DUMB-BELLS WITH YOUR PALMS FACING UPWARDS. RAISE YOUR ARMS UPWARDS UNTIL THEY MEET. THEN LOWER AND REPEAT THE EXERCISE.

5. To develop the muscles of your back, shoulders and the backs of your upper arms:

Sit on a chair or stool and hold a dumb-bell in each hand at shoulder height. Your palms should be facing forwards. Push your right hand up until your arm is fully extended. Lower and then repeat the exercise with your left hand. Lower and then repeat the exercise.

Mix and match

To get more fun out of your Trirobics endurance programme, try as many different types of endurance exercise as you can on different days of the week.

6. To develop the muscles of your forearm, wrist and hands:

a) Sit on a chair that has arms. Rest your forearms on the arm of the chair with your palms facing downwards. Keep your hand and wrist off the chair arm. Allow the dumb-bell to pull your hand downwards. Lift the dumb-bell in your right hand by using your wrist. Lower and repeat the exercise with your left hand. Lower and then repeat the exercise.

b) Do the same exercise with your palms facing upwards.

7 . To develop the muscles of your chest and upper arms:

A) *Lie on your back and hold your dumb-bells up in the air above you with your palms facing upwards and away from you. Lower the dumb-bells down to your chest and then raise them back up again. Repeat as often as you comfortably can.*

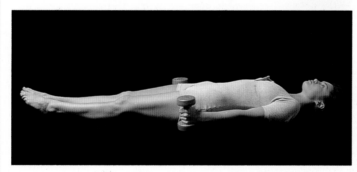

B) *Lie on your back and hold your dumb-bells up in the air above you with your palms facing upwards and away from you. Keeping your arms straight lower both dumb-bells to the floor. Lift the dumb-bells back up again and then repeat the exercise.*

8. TO DEVELOP THE MUSCLES AT THE SIDE OF YOUR BODY:

A) *STAND WITH YOUR FEET APART AND YOUR KNEES SLIGHTLY BENT. HOLD A DUMB-BELL IN YOUR RIGHT HAND AND LET IT HANG AT ARM'S LENGTH.*

B) *BEND TO THE RIGHT AS FAR AS YOU CAN. MOVE BACK TO THE UPRIGHT POSITION. BEND TO THE LEFT AS FAR AS YOU CAN. MOVE BACK TO THE UPRIGHT POSITION. SWAP THE DUMB-BELL TO YOUR OTHER HAND AND REPEAT THE EXERCISE.*

9. TO DEVELOP THE MUSCLES OF YOUR ABDOMEN:

LIE ON YOUR BACK WITH YOUR KNEES BENT AND YOUR FEET FLAT ON THE FLOOR. HOLD A DUMB-BELL ON YOUR CHEST WITH BOTH HANDS. TUCK YOUR CHIN INTO YOUR CHEST AND LIFT YOURSELF UP INTO A SITTING POSITION. LOWER YOURSELF SLOWLY. THEN REPEAT THE EXERCISE. YOU WILL FIND IT HELPS TO GET SOMEONE TO HOLD YOUR FEET.

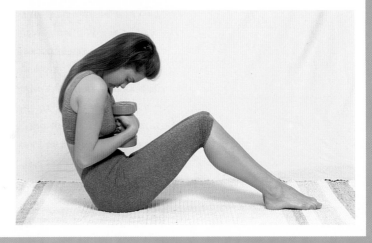

10. TO DEVELOP THE MUSCLES OF YOUR THIGHS:

STAND WITH YOUR FEET APART AND YOUR KNEES SLIGHTLY BENT. HOLD A DUMB-BELL IN EACH HAND WITH YOUR ARMS HANGING BY YOUR SIDES. KEEPING YOUR BACK STRAIGHT BEND YOUR KNEES UNTIL YOUR THIGHS ARE PARALLEL TO THE GROUND. RETURN TO THE STARTING POSITION AND THEN REPEAT THE EXERCISE.

WARNING

IT IS A MYTH THAT YOU NEED TO EXPERIENCE PAIN TO BENEFIT FROM EXERCISE. PAIN IS YOUR BODY'S WAY OF SAYING 'STOP'. IF YOU IGNORE A PAIN – OR TRY TO EXERCISE THROUGH IT – YOU WILL DO YOURSELF HARM.

11. TO DEVELOP THE MUSCLES OF YOUR CALVES:

STAND WITH YOUR TOES ON A THICK BOOK, YOUR KNEES SLIGHTLY BENT AND YOUR HEELS ON THE FLOOR. HOLD A DUMB-BELL IN EACH HAND WITH YOUR ARMS HANGING BY YOUR SIDES. LIFT YOUR HEELS OFF THE FLOOR AND THEN LOWER THEM BACK DOWN AGAIN. REPEAT THE EXERCISE.

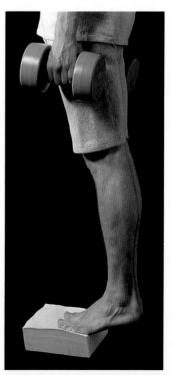

CHAPTER ELEVEN

Alternative Stress Therapies That Work

During the last few years an enormous number of alternative therapies have been promoted as useful for the treatment of stress-related disorders. Like orthodox remedies, some of them work and some of them don't, but unlike orthodox remedies, the associated side effects are usually mild and short-lived.

I have analyzed the best-known alternative stress remedies so that you can differentiate between the good, the bad and the simply ineffective.

"Alternative practitioners are, by and large, particularly good at dealing with anxiety, tiredness and stress-related disorders"

When choosing an alternative practitioner it is important to remember that not all the people who practise these various specialities are properly trained or qualified. The explosion of interest in alternative therapies has meant that in many specialities it is possible to obtain official-looking diplomas by post. In many parts of the world it is perfectly possible to become a qualified hypnotherapist by completing a mail order correspondence course and it is possible to become a 'qualified' acupuncturist by attending a two-day weekend course on the subject.

It is perfectly possible for someone with absolutely no training to leave a factory or office job on Friday evening, set up a consulting room, advertise in the local newspaper and open for business on the following Monday morning.

I believe that the best way to choose a reliable and effective alternative practitioner is by word of mouth. Ask your friends and relatives if they know of a good practitioner – and don't be afraid to ask your family doctor for a recommendation. Family doctors usually know which local practitioners are best, or how you should go about finding one – and most are happy to recommend good complementary practitioners in your area.

How to choose a good alternative practitioner

Do always remember that there are very few constraints governing the provision of alternative or complementary medical services. Some practitioners are reliable, well-trained, honest, ethical and honourable. Others are simply after your money.

The best way to choose a good local practitioner is by word of mouth. Ask your friends and relatives if they know of someone they can recommend. And don't be afraid to ask your family doctor for advice. The majority of doctors approve of their patients seeking help from alternative therapists and your doctor will probably know which local therapists are reliable and which are incompetent and unscrupulous.

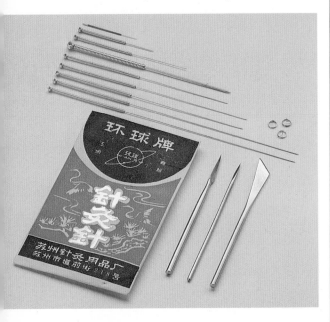

Acupuncture needles vary in diameter and length

The facts about acupuncture

Having a silver needle stuck in your skin to cure your arthritis may sound like a joke, but it isn't. Acupuncture is one of the oldest, best established forms of medical treatment in the world, and there is no doubt that it works.

Back street clinics and poorly trained practitioners may have given acupuncture a terrible image. But, done properly by a fully trained expert, it is a safe and remarkably effective technique.

Far-fetched as it may seem, acupuncture is reputed to have started when primitive warriors, injured by sharp enemy arrows, discovered that although their wounds were painful, their long-standing muscle and bone pains subsequently disappeared completely.

Deciding that there was a link between their injuries and the disappearance of what was undoubtedly early arthritis, the warriors learned how and where to prick themselves with sharp arrow heads to get rid of disabling pains.

Eventually, the science of acupuncture was born, and it slowly became more sophisticated. By the Bronze Age – two or three thousand years B.C. – they were using bronze acupuncture needles.

It was in China that acupuncture really developed – using needles made of gold, silver, wood, bamboo or even bone. The traditional Chinese believed that human life was controlled by an internal energy force which they called 'chi'. They claimed that this energy force flowed around the body along 12 main meridians or channels. If one of the channels got blocked then the flow of energy would stop or slow down and the individual would fall ill.

The practice of acupuncture is built upon the fact that there are around 1,000 acupuncture points around the body which can be used to tap into the internal energy force – rather in the way that oil pipeline engineers use entrance hatches to enable them to clear blockages in the pipes.

Before they attempt to free the flow of energy, skilled acupuncturists make a diagnosis in much the same sort of way that orthodox British doctors do. One of the most important parts of the physical examination is the taking of the pulse. Chinese acupuncture experts recognize 12 different pulses!

Today, acupuncture needles are usually made of stainless steel or copper. The needles vary in length from a fraction of an inch to seven inches. Their diameter is usually 1/17,000 in or 1/18,000 in. Obviously, it is important that the needles are properly sterilized between patients if the risk of transmitting hepatitis or AIDS is to be minimized.

Although choosing the correct acupuncture point is vital, it isn't just the site of insertion that is important. The angle at which the needle is inserted, the way it is moved around by twirling, pushing or pulling and the length of time it is left in position will all affect the final result. Some modern acupuncturists use electrical stimulation to activate the acupuncture needles.

Occasionally, acupuncturists use a technique known as moxibustion. This involves drying and shredding leaves of the Chinese wormwood plant and then burning the shredded leaves directly over an acupuncture point.

Moxibustion – a type of very localized hot poultice remedy – is said to 'tone' the body's vital energy flow and it is often used in the treatment of arthritis.

Just how acupuncture works is still a mystery. Some western scientists argue that it works by blocking channels which normally transmit pain impulses. Others claim that it stimulates the body to produce endorphins – natural, internal, painkilling hormones which are similar to morphine. Traditional acupuncturists simply say that it isn't necessary to understand how it works. All that matters is that it works.

Certainly there is little doubt that it often works well. Back in 1974 four American surgeons reported that they had treated over 300 patients in New York with acupuncture. They said that in over three quarters of the cases they found that it was one of the most effective cures for arthritis.

Over ten years ago, the World Health Organization concluded that 'the sheer weight of evidence demands that it must be taken seriously as a clinical procedure of considerable value'. The WHO listed a number of diseases that could be helped by a properly trained acupuncturist, including:

• **acute sinusitis and tonsillitis**
• **asthma and acute bronchitis**
• **toothache**
• **gastritis and ulcers**
• **headaches and migraines**
• **frozen shoulder and tennis elbow**
• **back pain**
• **arthritis**

There is little doubt that when acupuncture is done properly, by a fully trained acupuncturist, it can be both safe and effective – and particularly suitable for the treatment of a wide range of stress-related disorders.

Sadly, however, there are too many half-trained

amateurs around. Some practitioners – many of them doctors – have taken weekend courses in acupuncture and have given the speciality a bad name. Some have put patients' lives at risk.

Acupuncture is as complex as any other medical discipline. The World Health Organization claims that it is the continued scepticism of the medical establishment (often hand in hand with drug companies who for commercial reasons don't like the idea of acupuncture becoming popular) which has allowed the half-trained to do so much harm.

Certainly, a few years ago, when I was making a series of TV programmes on alternative remedies, an expert from the College of Traditional Chinese Acupuncture told me that he knew of patients who had needed to be admitted to mental hospitals after having had thoughtlessly administered acupuncture.

ACUPRESSURE: DO IT YOURSELF ACUPUNCTURE!

Some historians believe that when acupuncture meridians were first mapped out, practitioners did not use sharp needles but used their fingers instead. As with acupuncture, the aim is to restore the flow of energy along a meridian pathway, stimulating the flow when there is a blockage and bringing energy into the system when a meridian is empty.

In many ways acupressure is a mixture of acupuncture and massage – though there are also similarities to shiatsu. The acupressure therapist presses hard on specific parts of the patient's body, using only his or her finger tips – although there is a certain amount of controversy between therapists about the best places to stimulate in order to relieve specific symptoms. Because acupressure is simple and non-invasive, side effects are extremely rare.

Acupressure is very useful in the treatment of pain and all stress-related disorders. You can practise it yourself by following these tips:

1. Always use your finger tips and press quite hard.
2. The most effective acupressure points seem to be on or around your head and neck. By giving yourself a finger massage on the centre of your cheeks, on the outer edges of your eyes and on the centre of your forehead – between your eyes – it is

possible to relieve a wide range of symptoms.

3. To get rid of pain, try massaging the acupressure point in the fleshy web that lies between the thumbs and forefingers of both hands.

4. Medical scientists have shown that a stimulating massage just about anywhere on your body will help produce endorphins – calming and pain relieving hormones. So experiment wherever you can reach. But don't press anywhere that is in any way painful and never press on or around a site that seems infected, inflamed or injured.

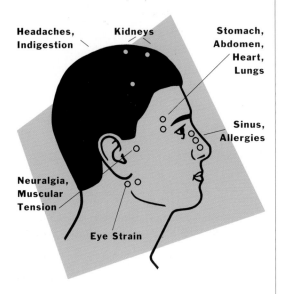

Above and below: some disorders which can be relieved by acupressure

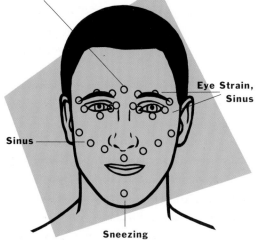

Massage has been popular for thousands of years and can be of far more value than most of us imagine. Massage can help ease tension, soothe tight muscles and relieve pain. Massage helps in several ways:

1. Massage helps to clear away the 'knots' that accumulate in your muscles when you are anxious, tense and under stress. Normally, when you feel tense, your muscles tighten as part of your body's natural response to stress: your body is getting you ready to fight or run away. Unfortunately, of course, most of our problems these days cannot be dealt with by a purely physical response and so the tensing of your muscles doesn't help at all. Worse still is the fact that, as your problems and stresses persist, so does your muscle tension. And as the tension persists, so your muscles stay tightly contracted and waste products such as lactic acid accumulate. These accumulated waste products make things even worse by making your muscles stiff and painful and preventing them from relaxing. It is most commonly the muscles in the neck, shoulders and back which seem to be affected by muscle tension and benefit most from massage. Massage helps to clear away the accumulated wastes and to relieve muscle stiffness remarkably effectively. A good massage can clear tight 'knots' out of muscles just as easily as it is possible to clear the wrinkles out of a bedsheet by gentle stroking.

2. The personal contact that is an inevitable part of a massage helps too. Most of us touch one another comparatively little. Social rules make it unacceptable to touch strangers in public and in some countries even friends or lovers are cautious about displays of physical affection. And yet there is much evidence to show that we *need* to be touched and cuddled by one another. Children who are not cuddled regularly as they are growing up develop all sorts of emotional problems. Gentle massage can help provide sympathy and reassurance which will eradicate tension and stress-induced muscle pains.

3. Massage helps to stimulate the production of endorphins – the body's internally produced pain relieving hormones.

4. Massage also stimulates the production of sensory impulses which then block the transmission of pain messages. The soothing feeling you get when someone massages your muscles means that pain messages simply cannot get through to your brain!

5. Some doctors and psychologists believe that by relaxing muscles through massage a masseur can also soothe the mind. Wilhelm Reich, a psychologist who practised at the turn of the century, believed that many people hide their emotions in their muscles and that there are strong links between the two. Just what the links consist of is a mystery but it is certainly true that many people do feel mentally relaxed and comfortable after a massage. Some people say they just want to go to sleep afterwards.

WHAT SORT OF MASSAGE?

FRICTION MASSAGE: INVOLVES RUBBING THE SKIN FAIRLY FIRMLY WITH THE FINGERS

TAPOTEMENT: BEATING, WHIPPING AND SLAPPING THE SKIN IN ORDER TO STIMULATE IT

EFFLEURAGE: SOOTHING, STROKING, MASSAGE MOVEMENTS DONE WITH THE FLAT OF THE HAND

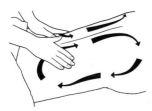

PETRISSAGE: PINCHING, KNEADING AND ROLLING THE SKIN

VIBRATION MASSAGE: DELICATE TAPPING AND CIRCLING OF THE SKIN

MASSAGE A FRIEND – OR BE MASSAGED BY ONE!

Although it can be extremely pleasant to have a massage from a professional you can get one from a friend or relative. For a good home massage follow these simple instructions:

1. Make sure that you are both completely comfortable. Any clothes you are wearing should be loose and light and the room temperature should be pleasantly warm. If the temperature is too low your muscles will contract and be stiff and difficult to massage. The room should not be too bright so use a small lamp for illumination. Many people find gentle background music helpful and relaxing.

2. A bed or sofa will be far too springy for a good massage so you should lie down on the floor. Spread a couple of rugs out on the carpet to make things more comfortable. If you are going to use oil or powder during the massage then spread an old sheet out underneath you to save making a mess.

3. If you are going to have the front of your body massaged, put one small cushion under your head and another under your knees. If you are going to have the back of your body massaged you won't need any cushions.

4. Remember that oil lubricates the skin and makes it much easier to give a massage. (Talcum powder is slightly less messy but works almost as well.) Ordinary baby oil will do just as well as anything more expensive.

5. The person giving the massage should start with a general massage – gently stroking and kneading *all* your muscles – before concentrating on those specific parts of your body which are particularly tense. Don't let anyone massage your joints or your spine – they should stick to muscles.

How to give yourself a massage!

If you haven't got a close friend to give you a massage, do not despair – you can give yourself one!

You won't be able to reach all the parts of your body but you should be able to reach enough of yourself to benefit enormously. Remember that when you automatically stretch an aching back or rub those parts of your body that ache, you are instinctively helping yourself through simple massage therapy.

If you have a headache or a painful, stiff neck, knead your shoulders and the back of your head with your fingers. You can get rid of a stress-related tension headache by massaging the area around the bridge of your nose just between your eyes, the areas to the side of your eyes and the areas just in front of your ears.

Next time you are washing your hair give your scalp a thorough massage with your finger tips. You will find it relaxing and soothing. You can massage your feet and hands easily, too. Simply work your way over your hands and feet, working your way inwards from the tips of your fingers and toes to the palm of your hands and the balls of your feet.

Get a cat!

Many people find that stroking a cat is particularly relaxing and soothing because when you stroke the cat you are inevitably stroking your hand at the same time – that stimulates the production of delicate nerve impulses which pass along the larger nerve fibres and block the passage of pain messages.

Since cats are warm creatures you will benefit from the heat of having a cat on your lap too!

How homeopathy can help you

The principles of homoeopathy go back to the origins of medicine but the principles of modern homoeopathy were established in the early part of the 19th century by Samuel Hahnemann, founded on laws devised by the Greek doctor and philosopher, Hippocrates. The latter claimed that if an individual who is suffering from an illness can be given a substance which will, in normal healthy individuals, cause symptoms similar to those produced by his illness then he will be cured.

Knowing that cinchona bark (which contains the drug we now know as quinine) relieves the symptoms of the ague (a disease now known as malaria), Hahnemann – who didn't have any symptoms of the ague – took some cinchona to see what effects it would have on him.

He was startled (but probably delighted) when, after taking the drug normally used to treat the ague, he developed the *symptoms* of the ague!

Moreover, when he stopped taking the drug the symptoms disappeared.

During the years that followed, Hahnemann experimented with all sorts of things – metals, animal products and vegetable substances – and discovered many other substances which could be used to produce symptoms similar to known disorders. By the time he died in 1843 Hahnemann had found 99 substances that seemed to work. Today homoeopaths use around 3,000 different substances varying from onions to gold, spiders to snake venom and Indian hemp to mercury.

Hahnemann also discovered that he didn't need to use large doses of his medicines in order to obtain the desired effects. Indeed, to the contrary, he discovered that the smaller the dose he used the more effective it was. It was in this way that Hahnemann developed the practice of modern homoeopathy.

Extremely small doses of drugs are given with the intention of triggering off a defensive reaction within the body and stimulating the body's natural ability to resist disease. (Homoeopathy has more than a little in common with vaccination – in which a small amount of an infective organism is introduced into the patient's body in order to provide protection by stimulating the body's defence mechanisms.)

There is still an enormous amount of controversy within the medical establishment about how or even whether homoeopathy really does work or whether the results are all 'in the mind', but the big advantage that homoeopathy has over other remedies is that side effects are relatively few and far between and dangerous side effects are virtually unheard of since the dosages which are used are so incredibly small.

You can buy homoeopathic remedies over the counter or you can consult a specialist homoeopath. If you do the former make sure that you buy from a reputable and well-informed pharmacist. If you decide to do the latter make sure that you visit a fully qualified practitioner.

AUTOGENIC TRAINING

In the 19th century two scientists working at the Berlin Neuro-Biological Institute discovered that some of their patients were able to put themselves into semi-hypnotic states. They also discovered that this condition had a positive, healing effect and they realized that patients who were able to calm and relax themselves were far less likely to need medical attention than patients who were constantly feeling anxious and under stress.

In the 1930s a German psychiatrist rediscovered this early German work and named it 'autogenic training'. It is still popular in Germany, though it is little known or used in the rest of the world.

Described by some observers as a Western version of yoga and transcendental meditation, autogenic training consists of six basic exercises. The patient repeats to himself the phrase which makes up each exercise until he is experiencing the suggested effect, then he goes on to the next step.

The six phrases used by autogenic practitioners are (with some slight variations):

1. My arms and legs are heavy…
2. My arms and legs are warm…
3. My heart is calm and regular…
4. My breathing is calm and regular…
5. My abdomen is warm…
6. My forehead is cool…

Although autogenic training is usually regarded as an 'alternative' form of medicine it was devised by doctors who had an orthodox training and there is, consequently, plenty of research evidence to show that autogenic training works. At the last count I knew of over 2,500 scientific publications proving that individuals who followed autogenic exercises benefited. The useful effects that are undoubtedly associated with its use are almost certainly due to the human body's innate capacity for self-healing.

Autogenic training is probably most suitable for individuals who need help to learn how to relax. Simpler and less formally structured self-healing techniques and relaxation exercises can probably be used with less professional support but anything that works is certainly worth recommending and autogenic training certainly works and has helped many thousands of stressed and anxious individuals.

The people who are most likely to be helped by autogenic training are probably the ones who find the simple, physical relaxation techniques (described in Chapter Eight) and the mental relaxation techniques (described in Chapter Nine) attractive but who, for one reason or another, are unable to learn or use these techniques by themselves.

HYPNOTHERAPY AND SELF-HYPNOSIS

Hypnotherapy fascinated the Egyptians several thousand years ago but it wasn't until Franz Mesmer developed the concept in the late 18th century that hypnosis and hypnotherapy really came of age.

The first evidence that hypnotherapy could really help patients came in 1847 when a surgeon called James Esdale reported that he had performed 300 major surgical operations in India using hypnosis as the only anaesthetic. His report might have attracted more attention had not the 19th century also seen the development of gas anaesthesia and drugs such as aspirin. As it was, hypnosis drifted into a quiet medical backwater.

During the last few decades, hypnosis has come back into fashion again and numerous people now claim that hypnotherapy is an excellent way of dealing with anxiety, stress, panic attacks and a wide range of stress-related disorders.

Popular though hypnotherapy has now become, it is clear that it is not necessary to visit a hypnotist in order to benefit. Indeed, since there are many 'quacks' and 'charlatans' with very modest training and qualifications practising as hypnotists and hypnotherapists, the only type of hypnosis I recommend is self-hypnosis – using the 'daydreaming' technique described on pages 73 to 74 of this book.

FINDING PEACE THROUGH MUSIC

Four thousand years ago Hindu doctors used to play soothing, gentle music while surgeons were operating. They used to play music on the wards too after they discovered that music helped people to relax and to get better quicker after treatment.

Only in the last few decades, however, have we relearned the truth about the healing power of music. Thirty years ago in Scotland a psychiatrist called Dr. Isaac Sclare used soft and peaceful music to help patients recover from a wide range of mental disorders. More recently an Italian doctor has demonstrated the value of various forms of music in the treatment of mental and emotional problems, while Drs. Borzecki and Zakrzewski of the Pain Clinic at the Warsaw Academy of Medicine have shown that music can be used to soothe and relieve pain.

From the evidence, it is now clear that music can be soothing and relaxing: it can cheer you up when you are sad; it can calm you down when you are feeling anxious or over excited and it can help you overcome despair and depression.

You don't even have to be conscious to benefit from music therapy. Playing a tape of pulsating sounds continuously helps ensure that premature babies stay alive while music can penetrate and benefit the mind that is deaf to conversation.

The sort of music you should choose depends entirely on your own personal taste.

Some people find classical music most relaxing. Others prefer hard rock music. Many seem to find soothing, traditional ballads most calming. Some like quiet guitar music, others prefer jazz. Some find cham-

ber music soothing while others relax most effectively while listening to opera. Many find that specially recorded 'relaxation' music is most effective.

A portable cassette recorder with a pair of headphones will enable you to enjoy your favourite music wherever you are, without annoying your neighbours. You are also likely to find it easier to 'lose' yourself in your music if you use headphones.

Finally, don't forget that you can benefit by playing music as well as just listening to it. The piano and the guitar seem to be the two instruments most likely to prove soothing and relaxing, though it doesn't really matter what instrument you use as the important thing is that *you* find it relaxing.

HERBAL REMEDIES – DO THEY WORK AND ARE THEY SAFE?

Herbalists can, with some justification, claim that theirs is one of the oldest branches of medicine.

Animals have instinctively used plants for thousands of years and so have human beings. I doubt if there has ever been a time when men have not used herbs to help heal themselves.

By the middle of the 19th century, at least 80 per cent of all medicines were derived from plants and herbalism had become practical pharmacology. Then came the revolution inspired by the development of the pharmaceutical industry. Today, in the middle of the modern 'chemical' era of drugs, only about one third of the drugs we use are plant based – although most of the world's largest companies still spend a considerable amount of money investigating plants and traditional herbal remedies in their search for new 'wonder' drugs.

If you have faith in traditional, herbal products you can either obtain your medicines from a herbalist (there are thousands of practising herbalists around the world today), or directly over the counter. The main problem is that since there are 350,000 known species of plants of which around 10,000 have known medicinal properties, it isn't always easy to decide which of all these herbs to use for which symptoms.

Indeed, this confusion and lack of consistency even affects the professionals. In one large book of herbalism I found a list of 21 substances recommended for the treatment of eczema. In another major herbal textbook I found 18 substances listed for the same condition. But only two of the plants on the second list appeared on the first list!

Nor is it true to say that herbal products are always safe. Herbal medicines can be as toxic as any other drugs and when herbal remedies are prepared unprofessionally there is an enormous risk of contamination. Sometimes even the professionals make mistakes and a few years ago a warning about a type of herbal tea made with comfrey leaves had to be issued when it was found that deadly nightshade leaves had been mixed in with the comfrey by mistake. Some of the herbal products used as 'natural tranquillizers' and 'sedatives' can produce quite severe side effects including headaches, giddiness, high blood pressure, skin problems, diarrhoea, hallucinations, nervousness and heart disease.

Finally, there is the problem that very little clinical research has been organized to assess modern herbal products, and so it is still difficult to say precisely which herbs are best for which symptoms. The only herbal product for which I have seen any clinical research evidence which convinced me is valerian – a traditional tranquillizer. Portugese researchers have shown that this herb is as effective a tranquillizer as one of the benzodiazepines – without the risk of addiction (see page 54). Some experts claim that the side effects said to be associated with valerian include giddiness, headaches, muscle spasms, excitability and hallucinations, although the only two side effects found by the Portugese researchers were a dry mouth and drowsiness. If you want to take a herbal tranquillizer then valerian could help – though do make sure that the version you take is pure, and follow the advice of your practitioner and the manufacturer.

Although there may not yet be very much objective and reliable clinical evidence available in support of their use for stress-related disorders other herbal products are popular with some practitioners.

The herbs that are used in the treatment of stress and stress-related disorders vary from country to country but some of the most popular and widely used remedies include chamomile, hops, Jamaican dogwood, lavender, lemon balm, passion flower and scullcap.

A medicine made from the flowers of wild chamomile is believed to be effective in the treatment of all types of restlessness and nervous tension, but many users regard it as particularly effective for problems of the digestive tract which have been caused by stress and anxiety. Remedies made from hops are also thought to be especially useful in the treatment of bowel problems which have been produced by tension and worry.

Jamaican dogwood (usually regarded as potentially one of the most poisonous of herbal remedies if used incorrectly) is used in the treatment of headaches, toothache and period pains as well as sleeplesness which has been caused by nervous tension.

Lavender, which grows throughout Europe, is used as both relaxant and a stimulant. Many people regard it as a useful tonic in the treatment of exhaustion, but it is also used for a wide range of nerve problems. Like chamomile and hops it is often regarded as particularly suitable for the treatment of digestive upsets caused by stress and anxiety.

Lemon balm is one of the most widely used herbs for the treatment of anxiety and tension. It is often drunk to relieve stomach problems caused by stress and many users claim that it helps them get through hectic and worrying days.

Passion flower is also often used in the treatment of nervous tension, irritability and restlessness.

I think it is important to point out that although these herbal remedies have in most cases been used for centuries in the treatment of anxiety and nervous disorders there is still little or no clinical evidence available to show exactly how effective or reliable they are. There is, however, no doubt that each herb has many enthusiastic supporters who have found them beneficial.

Hopefully, herbalists will soon introduce proper clinical trials for the products they favour. At the moment it is too easy for sceptical orthodox practitioners to complain that some herbal products have not yet been subjected to the sort of rigorous tests to which allopathic remedies are usually exposed.

Remember that you should never take any herbal remedy while already taking any other drug and you should always seek medical advice *immediately*, if you notice any side effects or unexpected symptoms. You must also follow the manufacturer's instructions.

CHAPTER TWELVE

How To Sleep Well Without Pills

The quality and quantity of your sleep is important. It is while you are asleep that your batteries are recharged. During the daytime millions of bits and pieces of information are fed into your brain, and sleeping gives it its only real rest.

If you don't get the amount of sleep you personally need then you will wake up tired, irritable, inefficient and depressed. Sleep gives your body a chance to rest, recharge its batteries and to rebuild its strength.

Tranquillizers and sleeping tablets are widely used for the treatment of stress-related insomnia. But it is now widely accepted that such drugs can produce many problems – including addiction and, paradoxically, sleeplessness (see Chapter Six, Why Drugs Are Not The Answer,

"Sleep gives your body a chance to recharge its batteries and to rebuild its strength"

pages 54 to 61). So, in this chapter I'll explain how you can sleep well without pills.

I will also deal with many of the night time problems that cause so many people so much worry and anxiety.

Cramps, restless legs, sleepwalking, dreams and nightmares can all destroy a good night's sleep and can all make the very thought of going to bed quite terrifying.

When sleep is disturbed a vicious circle develops. The less sleep you have the lower your resistance to stress will become and the more vulnerable you will be to new anxieties and pressures. If you do not sleep regularly, comfortably and well you will be far less capable of coping with the many thousands of outside pressures and daily stresses to which you will inevitably be exposed. Without sleep you will be far more likely to suffer from the many different physical and mental disorders which are associated with stress.

Learning how to sleep well is an essential part of stress-proofing your body.

First, you should try to decide *why* you cannot get to sleep. Stress is the most common cause – but it isn't the only cause of insomnia.

• If you are kept awake by worry, you need to learn how to relax – and you may need to deal positively with some of the problems that are worrying you. Re-read the advice on earlier pages of this book.

• If noise keeps you awake then try wearing ear plugs. You should be able to buy them at your local chemist's shop – they cost very little.

• If you are kept awake by pain, breathlessness – or any other symptoms – then ask your doctor for treatment for the problem.

• If you simply don't feel tired when you go to bed then maybe you are trying to get too much sleep. Some people only need five hours a night. Most of us need less sleep as we get older.

• If you feel hungry at night then have a bite to eat before you go to bed. And remember that people who are slimming usually get less sleep than usual. If you are on a diet make sure that your late night nibble is a low-calorie snack. Do not drink anything containing caffeine (e.g. tea or coffee) because caffeine will keep you wake. Try to avoid cigarettes which are also a stimulant.

• If your bed is uncomfortable then maybe you need a new one. Soggy or lumpy mattresses often keep people awake.

• If you have recently been prescribed pills by your doctor, ask him if the pills could be keeping you awake. And remember that if you have been taking tranquillizers or sleeping tablets for more than two weeks, they can cause sleeplessness. But do *not* stop taking them suddenly (see page 59).

• If your bedroom is too stuffy and you cannot breathe at night, improve the ventilation – e.g. by opening a window.

• If your bed is cold, invest in an electric blanket (but be sure to follow the manufacturer's instructions – and do not go to bed with the blanket on) or a hot water bottle.

• If you have difficulty in turning off your mind when you get into bed, read a book before you go to sleep – preferably something not too demanding.

HOW TO GET TO SLEEP

IF YOU CANNOT FIND A CAUSE FOR YOUR SLEEPLESSNESS TRY THIS SIMPLE BEDTIME SLEEP PROGRAMME.

1. HAVE A BRISK WALK FOR 10–15 MINUTES OR EXERCISE IN THE HOUSE IF YOU DON'T WANT TO GO OUTSIDE. YOU WILL SLEEP BETTER IF YOU ARE PHYSICALLY TIRED RATHER THAN JUST MENTALLY EXHAUSTED. IF YOU TRY TO GO TO BED DIRECTLY AFTER DOING PAPERWORK YOU WILL FIND THAT YOUR BRAIN WON'T STOP BUZZING: THE THINGS YOU HAVE BEEN THINKING ABOUT WILL INSIST ON POPPING INTO YOUR MIND.

2. WRITE DOWN ALL YOUR PROBLEMS AND WORRIES IN A NOTEBOOK.

3. TAKE A HOT WATER BOTTLE TO BED. YOU WILL SLEEP BETTER IF YOU ARE WARM.

4. LIE IN A WARM BATH FOR 15 MINUTES.

5. GO TO BED WITH A RELAXING BOOK THAT YOU KNOW YOU WILL ENJOY. DON'T GO TO BED WITH SOMETHING THAT WILL MAKE YOU THINK OR WORRY.

6. WHEN YOU ARE FEELING TIRED, CLOSE YOUR EYES AND TAKE YOURSELF OFF TO SOMEWHERE RELAXING, WARM AND BEAUTIFUL. IF YOU HAVE DIFFICULTY IN CREATING A PEACEFUL DREAM-LIKE SEQUENCE FOR YOURSELF, RE-READ MY 'DAYDREAM' SCENARIO ON PAGE 73.

7. IF YOU DO WAKE UP OR YOU DO HAVE DIFFICULTY IN GETTING TO SLEEP, DON'T JUST LIE THERE GETTING MORE AND MORE UPTIGHT. PICK UP YOUR BOOK AND READ ANOTHER COUPLE OF CHAPTERS.

HOW TO CUT DOWN THE AMOUNT OF SLEEP YOU NEED

Some people manage to get through their lives with very little sleep – as little as three or four hours a night. You can train yourself to do the same if you want to.

Astronauts – who need to stay awake for long hours – are trained to cut down the time they spend asleep to five hours a night.

They do this by gradually going to bed later and later and setting the morning alarm clock earlier and earlier. They aim to cut one hour off at a time.

Research has shown that if you do this slowly then neither your physical nor your mental health will suffer. Your body will simply learn to make better use of shorter amounts of sleep.

THE BEDTIME JERK

Just before falling properly asleep it is common – and quite normal – to have a sudden muscle spasm. This is known as a myoclonic jerk and although it is unpleasant it is nothing to worry about.

The jerk may be accompanied by a feeling of falling or an imaginary loud noise. The jerk – produced by the spasm of relaxing muscles – may be so severe that the sufferer clutches for support to the bed.

Although a 'bedtime jerk' can leave the heart pounding it is unlikely to produce any lasting damage.

SLEEPWALKING

Sleepwalking can occur at any age – though it is perhaps most common among children. It tends to run in families and to affect men more than women.

It is *not* true that sleepwalkers cannot injure themselves. Stories about sleepwalkers falling out of windows without hurting themselves are quite false. Similarly, stories of sleepwalkers managing to walk along incredibly narrow ledges are invariably apocryphal.

If you have a sleepwalker in your family make sure that all doors and windows are firmly locked and cannot be opened automatically.

TALKING IN YOUR SLEEP

Most people talk occasionally in their sleep – usually about simple daytime problems that have worried them and stuck in their mind.

RESTLESS LEGS SYNDROME

Many women complain that while they lie in bed at night their legs twitch. This is different to the 'bedtime jerk' and is called the 'restless legs syndrome'.

It is one of the oldest of all disorders and was first described over 300 years ago. Caffeine is believed to be one of the major causes today.

To avoid the problem try drinking less – or weaker – coffee or tea. If you spend much of your time sitting down then mild exercise will probably help.

CRAMP

People often wake up at night with cramp in their lower legs. The pains are usually thought to be caused by the collection of waste products in the muscles which have collected there because of poor circulation.

To avoid cramp you should make sure that your bedclothes are not too tight around your feet – and avoid wearing tight stockings, socks or garters. You can try this stretching exercise, too: stand barefoot one yard away from a wall. Lean forwards until your hands touch the wall but keep your heels on the floor. Maintain this position for ten seconds and then repeat it once. Do this exercise three times a day for a week and then nightly before you get into bed.

HOW MUCH SLEEP DO WE NEED?

It varies according to age and from person to person. Babies need from eight to 16 hours a night – sometimes even more. Adults need between three and ten hours' sleep a night. The average is seven to eight hours. Most of us tend to need less sleep as we get older.

WILL LOSING SLEEP DO ME ANY HARM?

Not really, although if you stay awake for several days you may start to have hallucinations. If you have lost a night's sleep then you ought to try to get an extra three hours' sleep the following night – or soon after to help your body catch up. You only need to replace approximately one in three hours of lost sleep. (It seems likely that people who manage on just three or four hours' sleep a night have managed to eradicate the 'unnecessary' sleep hours.)

SLEEP FACT ONE Too much sleep makes you groggy and impairs your skills. An experiment with 12 volunteers who were allowed to sleep longer than usual showed that people who oversleep become less efficient when performing skills requiring thought and skill.

SLEEP FACT TWO A survey of 5,000 Californians showed that people who routinely sleep for less than six hours a night are 1.3 times as likely to die as people who sleep for seven or eight hours a night. (On the other hand people who sleep less gain several hours of 'living' every night!)

SLEEP FACT THREE Scientists have extracted a special SLEEP factor – consisting of glutamic acid, alanine, diaminopimelic acid and muramic acid – as the substance produced in the human brain during sleep. It is believed that eventually it will be possible to induce sleep by giving patients a tablet containing the SLEEP factor.

At the moment the snag is that to get enough SLEEP factor to make just *one* tablet would take 4.5 tons of human urine!

SLEEP FACT FOUR Most people wake up at night. Young adults wake up twice a night on average. Older people wake up an average of seven times a night.

SLEEP FACT FIVE Most adults take around ten minutes to fall asleep. But by the time we reach the age of 70 it usually takes us 20 minutes to fall asleep.

SLEEP FACT SIX If you learn something just before you go to sleep you are more likely to remember it. But it is a myth that you can learn by listening to tapes while you are asleep.

SLEEP FACT SEVEN When 18 middle-aged volunteers of both sexes – who all considered themselves to be poor sleepers – were put to sleep in a laboratory, it was found that they took only seven minutes longer than good sleepers to fall asleep. A man who claimed he hadn't slept for ten years was fast asleep for several hours, and a woman who said she never slept, slept soundly for five consecutive nights.

WHAT DO YOUR DREAMS MEAN?

Most of us dream – usually several times a night. But although you can often recollect your dreams quite clearly you probably have no idea what they mean.

That's a pity. Because your dreams can tell you a great deal about yourself, and understanding your dreams can help you combat anxiety, conquer stress and avoid depression.

When you go to bed tonight you'll probably lie awake for a few minutes. Don't worry about this – most people do it. Once you've become drowsy you'll fall into a predictable sleep pattern.

To begin with you'll drift into a light sleep, then you'll go into a deep sleep that will last for nearly an hour. During an average night you'll go through this pattern five times. But before each new sleep cycle your brain will buzz and for between ten and 30 minutes you'll be in 'dreamland' – an insane, unstructured world where there are no constraints and no rules and where nothing is impossible. Your body will be very relaxed but your brain will be buzzing.

This type of sleep is known as paradoxical sleep, or Rapid Eye Movement (REM) sleep for the simple reason that while you are in it your eyes will move more rapidly below your closed lids. There are several other physical changes which characterise REM sleep, the most important one is that your heart will beat faster. It is during the hours spent in REM sleep that you enter 'dreamland'.

In your dreams you may be able to fly and walk through walls; but you may also be unable to run when threatened and unable to call out when you need help.

Freud claimed that during our dreams our unconscious minds express hidden doubts and desires. He believed that most dreams are driven by sexual fears.

But today it's clear that when psychologists and psychoanalysts try to read dreams they can get it badly wrong and produce wildly misleading results.

The person who is best equipped to read *your* dreams is *you*. By studying your dreams carefully you should be able to learn a great deal about your ambitions, your hopes and your fears.

Here, to help you, are the 20 most common questions people ask about dreams:

Q I NEVER DREAM. WHY?

A You only *think* you don't dream. You do. We're only aware of our dreams – and only able to remember them – if we happen to wake up while we're in 'dreamland'. If you regularly wake up when you are in deep or light sleep you'll be unaware of what happened when you were dreaming.

Q HOW CAN I MAKE SURE I DO WAKE UP WHEN I'M DREAMING – SO THAT I'LL BE ABLE TO REMEMBER A DREAM?

A Vary the time when you wake up – but go to bed at the same time. This way you'll greatly increase your chances of waking up during or just after a dream. Keep a notebook and pencil by the side of your bed so that you can write down as much of your dream as you can – as quickly as possible. As soon as you get up out of bed your dream will quickly disappear.

Q DO SLEEPING TABLETS MAKE YOU DREAM MORE?

A Yes.

Q WHAT SORT OF PEOPLE DREAM MOST?

A Fat people dream more than thin people. And women dream more than men: 45 per cent of women say that they dream several times a night but only 34 per cent of men say they dream that often.

Q I OFTEN HAVE VERY SEXY DREAMS. DOES THAT MEAN THAT I'M A SEX MANIAC?

A No. An astonishing 86 per cent of men and 72 per cent of women have sexy dreams. Some are erotic, some are romantic and some are outrageously and unashamedly pornographic. One very respectable lady told her doctor that she regularly dreamt that she took part in sex orgies with members of her husband's soccer team. The orgies lasted all night and the woman said that during each dream she had sex with every member of the soccer team – except her husband. This woman's dream was inspired simply by sexual frustration. In real life she had a tricky pregnancy and had been told not to have sex with her husband to avoid damaging her baby. So, in 'dreamland' she sought satisfaction from every man except her husband.

Q I SOMETIMES DREAM THAT I AM BEING RAPED. THIS WORRIES ME. WHAT DOES IT MEAN. I KNOW I WOULDN'T ENJOY BEING RAPED.

A You are struggling to balance your natural sexual urges with attitudes towards sex that you learned from parents and teachers. In 'dreamland' you are having sex – and enjoying it – without having to take responsibility for your actions.

Q IS IT POSSIBLE FOR ME TO CHOOSE WHAT I DREAM ABOUT?

A Yes. As you fall asleep make sure that the last thing on your mind is the scene or person you want to dream about. But be warned! Although you can – to a certain extent – plan the basic content of a dream it is impossible to decide exactly what is going to happen. Your plans for a night of romantic passion could easily turn into something else . . .

Q I OFTEN DREAM THAT I'M FLYING. DOES THIS HAVE ANY SIGNIFICANCE?

A It could have, though there are many variations on this theme. Some people dream of flying after falling off a cliff, others of flying after falling out of an aeroplane and yet others of flying after falling out of windows. Some experts claim that 'flying' dreams signify sex. If the flying makes you nervous then you are nervous about sex. If you really enjoy the flying then you enjoy sex and want more of it in your life. But there are other possible explanations. Maybe you dream of flying because your career is about to 'take off'. Or it may be, if you dream of falling a lot, that you feel that your life is getting out of control.

Q I DREAM A LOT ABOUT BEING FOUND NAKED IN PUBLIC. IT IS ALWAYS VERY EMBARRASSING. WHAT DOES THIS MEAN?

A This is a very common dream. People suddenly find themselves wandering naked about the street. Or they dream that they are naked at a party. Everyone looks down on them. Dreams of this kind suggest that you feel incompetent or inferior. If you can identify the people who are looking down on you then those are probably the people you feel inferior to.

Q IN MY DREAMS I OFTEN GO BACK IN HISTORY AND FIND MYSELF TAKING PART IN A COSTUME DRAMA! WHAT CAN THIS MEAN?

A You probably feel unhappy with your life. And you may feel that life in another age might be more fun, more romantic or more exciting.

Q DO DREAMS EVER PREDICT THE FUTURE?

A Thousands of people have claimed that they've seen the future in their dreams. Most are dismissed as mad. But a growing number of scientists now believe that premonitions – either when you are awake or when you are in 'dreamland' may be just as 'real' as other senses. But if you regularly have horrible dreams about terrible things happening to you or those you love, be reassured by the fact that you are almost certainly not dreaming about things that are going to happen but about things that you are worried about happening.

Q THE QUEEN APPEARS A LOT IN MY DREAMS. WHY? I HARDLY EVER THINK ABOUT ROYALTY WHEN I AM AWAKE.

A How do you respond to her in your dreams? The Queen almost certainly represents someone who plays an important role in your life. And the way you respond to her in your dreams reflects the way you feel about that person. Were you frightened of her? Or did you get on well with her? It shouldn't be too difficult to identify the person you are seeing as the Queen. It will probably be a boss or some other individual in a position of authority.

Q I'M ALWAYS MISSING TRAINS IN MY DREAMS. CAN YOU EXPLAIN IT?

A It may mean that you are involved in something that you don't really have faith in. It may mean that you really want to get away from your current responsibilities – but cannot. Incidentally, once you start catching the train with any regularity that probably means that your confidence is increasing – and that you have real faith in your plans for the future.

Q I DREAM ABOUT DEATH A LOT AND IT WORRIES ME.

A It shouldn't. A dream about death may simply signify that you are looking forward to something that is about to happen in your life – a new job or a new relationship for example.

Q I OFTEN DREAM ABOUT BEING AT A PARTY AND HAVING A REALLY GOOD TIME. ITS A VERY ENJOYABLE DREAM BUT I'D LIKE TO KNOW WHAT IT MEANS.

A If you are having a good time but everyone else is standing or sitting around looking a bit fed up or left out of things, then maybe you are subconsciously aware that you are behaving greedily. Maybe you are taking too much out of life – and not putting enough back in. If, in your 'dreamland' party, you were having a rotten time but everyone else was enjoying themselves, then the explanation would probably be that you were getting a raw deal. In 'dreamland' food and drink often represent emotional needs rather than physical ones.

Q I OFTEN DREAM OF TV STARS. WHAT DOES THAT MEAN?

A It may mean that you want your life to be more exciting. Your dream may be merely a simple 'escape'. But how did you get on with the star? If you got on well with them that usually signifies that your confidence is high. If you felt very inferior then your confidence probably needs a boost.

Q WATER ALWAYS PLAYS A PART IN MY DREAMS. CAN YOU EXPLAIN WHY?

A It may be that you dream of water because you are afraid of it, but it's just as likely that the water is irrelevant, and it is what is happening on, or in, the water that is more important.

Q MAGGOTS OFTEN APPEAR IN MY DREAMS. THERE ARE MILLIONS OF THEM AND THEY ARE HORRIBLE. WHAT ON EARTH CAN BE THE EXPLANATION?

A Writhing maggots usually suggest that there is something in your life that is rotten. Maybe you have some guilty, hidden secret. Maybe there is a scandal waiting to be exposed.

Q I DREAM ABOUT BEING BURIED ALIVE. WHAT ON EARTH DOES THAT MEAN?

A You are probably being 'buried' by your daily responsibilities and burdens. Maybe you feel repressed or over-dominated by some individual. You need to think hard about your life to find the answer.

CHAPTER THIRTEEN

How To Cope With Panic Attacks

Occasionally anxiety seems to get out of control. If you have ever had a panic attack then you will know that the name is very apt. At least one in 50 people suffer from panic attacks and as many as one in eight students or children may suffer from them. Panic attacks run in families and ruin thousands of peoples' lives.

These attacks – which can be horrifying – are usually a sign that anxiety is getting out of control. The initial symptoms vary but can include: feeling faint, sweating, being short of breath, having a pounding heart, getting butterflies in the stomach, an inability to concentrate, shaking and trembling, palpitations, headache and a dry mouth.

Panic attacks may be triggered by chemicals and drugs such as caffeine – found in tea, coffee and cola. Or they may be caused directly by stress.

In America, researchers at Washington University in St. Louis, Missouri, told human guinea pigs that they would receive electric shocks at some time in the future. The human guinea pigs were also told that the longer the shocks were delayed the worse the shocks would be when they came. Not surprisingly, the volunteers became increasingly anxious – and eventually they developed panic attacks.

Clearly, therefore, one important cause of panic attacks must be the build up of anxiety over a period of time. The best way to stop panic attacks is to prevent anxiety building up.

Nine out of ten panic attacks can be prevented. One of the best ways to do this is by taking regular gentle exercise. Regular exercise (see Chapter Ten) can help in three ways – by reducing muscle tension, by reducing the heart rate and stress hormone levels.

Alternatively, you should be able to prevent panic attacks interfering with your life by learning how to relax your body and your mind by using the advice in Chapters Eight and Nine.

If, despite a suitable panic prevention programme, a panic attack develops you should be able to eradicate the symptoms by breathing as slowly and as deeply as you can to slow down your body – and get your panic symptoms under control.

CHAPTER FOURTEEN

How To Harness Positive Emotions And Conquer Negative Ones

However careful you are to organize your life so that your exposure to unnecessary stress is kept to a minimum, and however skilled you are at maximizing your ability to withstand stress and cope with pressure, there will always be moments when stress overwhelms your defences.

At those moments your natural tendency will probably be for you to respond not in any sensible, logical, analytical way but to respond instinctively and emotionally. Depending on the nature of the stress (and the way you feel about it), you may want to cry, shout, laugh or be plunged into deep despair.

"...your natural tendency will probably be for you to respond not in any sensible, logical, analytical way but to respond instinctively and emotionally"

In practice, however, things are not quite this straightforward and natural responses aren't always the responses other people see. Superficially your emotional responses may seem automatic and quite beyond voluntary control and you may think that when stress makes you sad you will cry, and when anxieties make you angry you will shout, but the relationship between stress and your emotions isn't that simple. Often your emotional responses to any given situation will be governed either by behavioural patterns which you learned many years before from parents, teachers and friends, or as a result of prejudices from people in authority or from people you respected. As a result you will subconsciously allow each natural, healthy response to be dominated and controlled by an intellectual response. Instead of crying, you may stiffen your upper lip; instead of shouting, you may simply turn away and nurse your anger inside you.

Although this intellectual over-ride may have a certain social value (preventing you from making a fool of yourself in public), it will do your health no good at all and it will dramatically increase the chances of stress eventually having a devastating effect on your physical and mental well-being.

The contrary truth is that the more you learn how to give full reign to your emotions – whether they are positive ones or negative ones – the better you will be able to protect yourself against stress-related damage and the happier and healthier you will be.

As I have already explained, the vast majority of all the illnesses from which we suffer these days, are caused by stress and all illnesses are made worse by stress. Our minds are killing us and making us pretty ill as they do it. Worry, anxiety, stress and pressure can cause an enormous amount of agony and real pain.

The opposite is also true. Just as negative thinking, unhappy thoughts and genuine problems can all make us ill, so, positive thinking, happy thoughts, love, companionship and support can all help to keep us healthy and help us to get better when we are ill.

If you stop and think about it all, this makes good sense. After all, if your mind can make you ill then surely it is only fair that it should also be able to make you well again.

Over the last few years, some remarkable pieces of scientific work have been done by doctors keen to investigate the ways in which a positive approach can help to heal real illness. For example, consider this simple experiment which a doctor performed with 200 of his patients – all of whom had symptoms but none of whom had definable illnesses.

The doctor divided the patients into two main groups. The patients in the first group were treated politely but were not given any firm assurance by the doctor about when they would get better. The patients in the second group were told confidently that they would be better in a few days time.

When the doctor next saw his patients he noticed a remarkable difference between the two groups. Nearly two thirds of the patients who had been given positive encouragement had got better whereas only just over a third of the patients who had been given no encouragement had recovered.

LAUGHTER IS THE BEST MEDICINE

It may sound corny but it is true – laughter *is* the best medicine. When you laugh, your whole body benefits: your lungs are exercised and your heart is given excellent 'tuning up' exercise. More importantly, special healing hormones are released inside your body. After a good laugh your blood pressure will be lower, your breathing will be easier and you will sleep better.

Even simply smiling can help make you feel calmer and more relaxed. You will find that you benefit from

Funny films can help you deal with stress and protect your body from stress-related illness

smiling in two quite specific and separate ways.

First, you will benefit because when you smile at people they like you. They may not know why. They may not *want* to like you, but they will feel themselves warming to you. They will want to please you and see more of your smile so they will do things which you like. Everyone wants to please other people – it is a natural and entirely understandable human emotion. A smile is the key that unlocks happiness. Watch a mother with her baby. Watch two lovers. Watch a good salesman with a customer. They all smile.

Second, if you smile *you* will feel better, too. Nothing conquers sadness, boredom or irritation quite so effectively as a smile. Try it. Try putting a really cheerful smile on your face. You will find it difficult to stay quite so sad and you will *feel* your eyes beginning to sparkle with laughter.

Put more laughter into your life by, for example, trying not to take yourself too seriously. You don't have to be pompous to get the respect of other people. Try to listen to yourself occasionally when you're talking and try to see yourself as others see you.

Spend as much time as you possibly can with cheerful people. If you spend all your time with people who have long faces and who always look on the black side then you will eventually acquire a gloomy disposition yourself. Depression, like measles, is contagious. Bright and cheerful friends will help to make you bright and cheerful too. People who make you smile and laugh will make you healthier as well as happier.

Make a list of your favourite funny books and films. Keep a few of them around to cheer you up when you're feeling glum. And don't be afraid to play with children's toys occasionally if they cheer you up. One businessman I know reads boys' comics on the train – hidden inside his copy of the financial paper. He says they make him laugh and relax after a hard day's work. But take care: not all types of humour will improve your health. As a general rule, the best type of humour is simple, straightforward clownish comedy or slapstick. There is a chance that satirical or cynical comedy will increase your chances of becoming ill. Humour that makes fun of particular groups of people or that makes you feel uncomfortable is more likely to make you ill than to improve your health.

Crying is a healthy response to stress; Australian Prime Minister Bob Hawke breaks down on television

CRYING ISN'T WIMPY

Millions of men regard crying as something only women should do. Politicians and sportsmen who have cried in public after defeat or even in passion or anger often find that their careers are ruined and that they are regarded with a mixture of distaste, embarrassment and contempt by others. In many countries boys who cry are scolded and are told by their fathers that they should never allow their emotions to show. Today even some women regard crying as a sign of weakness.

This is a tragic mistake for crying is an essential and very healthy way of dealing with unhappiness. People who do not allow themselves to cry are depriving themselves of an important and effective release valve. Crying is a natural and useful response to difficult, frustrating or annoying circumstances. People who never cry are making life more difficult for themselves and are increasing their own chances of suffering from serious physical or mental disease. People who refuse to cry and keep their emotional feelings locked up inside themselves are more likely to end up suffering from mental disorders such as depression and physical disorders as serious as heart disease or high blood pressure.

It is no coincidence that British men, who generally

regard crying as quite unacceptable, have a high chance of suffering from and dying from heart disease.

Crying helps in several ways. Obviously, when we cry it is clear that we need support, succour and encouragement - and so we are more likely to be provided with those essentials by those who are close to us.

In addition there is now clear scientific evidence which shows that crying is good for us because it helps our bodies to get rid of chemicals which, if they are allowed to accumulate, can do us harm. The tears which we produce when we are miserable are quite different to the tears which we produce when our eyes are merely irritated by the wind. When we cry because we are sad our tears contain a chemical; if we don't cry that chemical will accumulate and will, in the end, be likely to lead to a proper, fully blown depression.

EVERYBODY NEEDS SOMEBODY

Everyone needs someone to cuddle, to hold, to talk to, to be with and to share problems with. Being alone is OK for fridges and filing cabinets, but people need loving – and lots of it.

The power of being loved and cared for is so strong that I have no doubt that I could slash drug bills if I could prescribe a cuddle every evening and a kiss every morning for every man, woman and child in the world.

Insurance companies have discovered that a morning kiss can dramatically reduce your chances of having a car accident on the way to work. A kiss from someone who cares is a vaccination against stress – it's a reminder that you aren't entirely alone in the world.

A woman – or man – who gets a daily kiss and cuddle will, on average, live five years longer than a woman – or man – who doesn't. Without regular kisses and cuddles, children become emotionally unstable and exceptionally susceptible to fear, stress and pressure. Old people who live alone and who are friendless and uncared for suffer far more from physical and mental illness – and are far more likely to die – than old people who have good friends.

The healing power of a good cuddle is so well-established that in some hospitals today, double beds are provided so that partners can provide their own special healing treatments.

If you're single then you are in a high risk category. You are more likely to suffer from a stress-related illness and you're more likely to die early.

But you can change the odds dramatically in your favour by finding a good friend.

It does *not* have to be a sexual partner. All you need in your life is someone who *cares* for you, a friend or member of your family – someone whom you can love and care for in return. Loving – and being loved –

works because it makes us realize that we are not alone.

The modern world is a lonely, frightening place. It's easy today for people to suffer through being alone.

I get lots of letters from people who aren't really ill: they're just lonely. They don't need pills; they need loving. And the bottom line is that we should all cherish our friends, for it is friendship – not sexual love – that gives us all real support, encouragement and strength.

If you have friends in your life who love and care for you, then you will be able to face illness with strength and adversity with hope. Friendship will illuminate the darkest moments of your life.

Real wealth is measured not in material possessions but in love and friendship.

LEARN TO DEAL WITH ANGER IN A POSITIVE WAY

You, like everyone else, will get angry from time to time. Anger is a perfectly natural and reasonably healthy response to stressful circumstances. Anger only becomes a destructive and dangerous problem when it is allowed to build up inside you and it is no sin at all to acknowledge the existence of your anger and to let it out occasionally.

If you feel yourself getting angry ask yourself whether or not the matter is worth getting angry about and whether or not your anger is justified. If your answer to both these questions is 'yes', then don't suppress your anger or try to hide it: let it out. If you feel your anger building up inside you and you feel tempted to get rid of your anger in some direct, physical way, then follow your natural instincts as much as possible.

I am not, of course, suggesting that you race round and hit anyone who has annoyed you. That would not be very practical. But you can get rid of your excess anger in any number of simple but effective ways. Some people get rid of their anger by playing sport or working out in the gym. They claim that by hitting a tennis ball or a squash ball they can get rid of some of their anger in a harmless way (though if you allow your anger to interfere you shouldn't expect to play too well!). Even in and around the house there are ways to get rid of anger: different people find different things satisfying. Some, for example, find that gardening or chopping wood is therapeutic.

THE ADVANTAGE OF LOOKING ON THE BRIGHT SIDE

When I was in my final year at medical school everyone was under tremendous pressure to pass their exams. I will never forget how two student friends of mine reacted to this pressure.

One, (I'll call him Jack), was very pessimistic. He was convinced that he would fail his exams. The other, (I'll call him Chris), was wildly optimistic. He had a happy-go-lucky attitude. He didn't work very hard but he thought he would pass.

Jack passed his exam and Chris failed; but neither of them responded to these results in the way that you might have expected.

Jack remained pessimistic about the future and started to worry about his first job as a doctor. Chris, on the other hand, remained remarkably optimistic – even though he had to spend another six months as a student. 'It'll mean that I can delay paying income tax for a bit longer,' he laughed.

That was 20 years ago.

Recently, I got in touch with both Jack and Chris to see how they were getting on.

Jack is now an important hospital consultant. He has troublesome and dangerous high blood pressure and has already had his first warning of heart trouble. He worries constantly about anything and everything.

Chris is a family doctor. He is as carefree and as optimistic as ever. He enjoys life to the full. And, although he is overweight and drinks too much, he is in relatively good health.

Not all people can be clearly defined as 'optimists' or 'pessimists' but most people are mainly one thing or the other. Pessimists tend to look on the black side and to suffer from terrible health, whereas optimists generally put their failures behind them, do their best to look on the bright side and usually enjoy very good health.

If you are a natural pessimist you won't be able to change your personality and turn yourself into a dedicated optimist. But it will, however, be perfectly possible for you to dilute your natural pessimism with a healthy splash of optimism. Instead of always dwelling on the gloomy aspects of every situation, try to think positively. Although it won't always be possible, try to find the 'silver lining' in as many situations as possible.

STRESS INDEX

PHOTOGRAPHIC ACKNOWLEDGEMENTS

The photographs in this book are from the following sources:

Allsport, London: Tony Duffy 76, C. Matos 65, Mike Powell 63;

Kobal Collection, London 64, 122;

Mirror Australian Telegraph Publications, Surry Hills, NSW 123;

Reed International Books: Peter Chadwick 102,

Rex Features Limited, London 15:

Patrick Durand/Sipa Press 12, Malanca/Sipa Press 7;

Spectrum Colour Library, London 72;

Tony Stone Photolibrary, London: Paolo Negri 47,

Andre Perlstein 2, 121, Chad Slattery 71;

ZEFA, London 14, 74, 119: Stockmarket 17.

SPECIAL PHOTOGRAPHY

Richard Truscott 4, 10, 11, 22, 24, (all four), 29, 55, 67,
75, 77, 79, 82, 83, 85, 91 (all six), 92 left and right,
93 (all four), 99, (all four), 101, 111, 124.

ILLUSTRATION

Kevin O'Keefe 35.

Robin Heighway - Bury 43.

LINE ARTWORK

Jared Gibey 41, 104, 105.

Simon David 115, 116, 117.

DESIGN/ART DIRECTION Sarah Pollock

EDITOR Sian Facer

PRODUCTION Alison Myer

PICTURE RESEARCH Judy Todd